WE GOOD...WE NO SHOOT

The Christmas Truce at Plugstreet Wood in 1914

Front cover: 1. *The Illustrated London News 9th January 1915*
British

2. *One*
from a
©201

azine

Published by Dene House Publishing
Dene House, Walton, Warwick. CV35 9HX
www.meetatdawnunarmed.co.uk

Designed by Ruth Smith, Damson Creative Ltd.
www.damsoncreative.co.uk

Printed and bound in Malta on behalf of Latitude Press Ltd.
www.latitudepress.co.uk

ISBN 978-0-9561820-3-6

Opposite page: Plugstreet Wood - from Bullets and Billets
by Bruce Bairnsfather
© *2014 Estate of Barbara Bruce Littlejohn*

WE GOOD...WE NO SHOOT

The Christmas Truce at Plugstreet Wood in 1914

by
Andrew Hamilton
and
Alan Reed

CONTENTS

FOREWORD   Tonie and Valmai Holt 9

INTRODUCTION   'A DAY UNIQUE IN THE WORLD'S HISTORY' 11

ABBREVIATIONS   15

COMPOSITION OF THE BRITISH EXPEDITIONARY FORCE (B.E.F.) 16

"PLUGSTREET WOOD". 17

TRENCHES AND MANNING ROUTINES FOR THE 10th and 11th BRIGADES 21

DECEMBER 1914   24

CHRISTMAS EVE   34

CAROLS, CONCERTINAS and MOUTH ORGANS on CHRISTMAS EVE. 41

CHRISTMAS DAY   44

EXCHANGES   48

COMMUNICATION   51

GERMANS   52

FOOTBALL   54

CHRISTMAS FAYRE   58

STRANGE HAPPENINGS AND COINCIDENCES 59

GROUP PHOTOGRAPHS. 62

INTELLIGENCE GATHERING. 64

"MAKING GOOD"   66

COLLECTION OF BODIES AND BURIALS 67

BOXING DAY   70

27th to 30th DECEMBER 71

NEW YEAR   74

REACTIONS   77

OFFICIAL REACTIONS 83

CONCLUSION $\cdots\cdots\cdots\cdots\cdots\cdots\cdots\cdots\cdots\cdots$ 85

APPENDICES:

I   SOME OF THOSE WHO PARTICIPATED: $\cdots\cdots\cdots\cdots\cdots$ 88

    Captain Robert Hamilton, 1/ Royal Warwicks $\cdots\cdots\cdots\cdots$ 88

    Lieutenant Guy Cave, 1/ Royal Warwicks $\cdots\cdots\cdots\cdots$ 89

    Serjeant A.H. Cook, 1/ Somerset Light Infantry $\cdots\cdots$ 91

    Lieutenant Bruce Bairnsfather, Machine-Gun officer in 1/ $\cdots\cdots$ 93
    Royal Warwicks

II   THE CEMETERIES and THE MEMORIAL
    IN THE PLUGSTREET AREA $\cdots\cdots\cdots\cdots\cdots\cdots$ 96

III A TOUR OF THE CEMETERIES OF PLUGSTREET WOOD $\cdots\cdots$ 99

IV CHRISTMAS TRUCES AFTER 1914 $\cdots\cdots\cdots\cdots\cdots$ 107

ACKNOWLEDGEMENTS $\cdots\cdots\cdots\cdots\cdots\cdots\cdots\cdots$ 109

ARCHIVES, LIBRARIES and MUSEUMS $\cdots\cdots\cdots\cdots\cdots$ 110

OFFICIAL SOURCES $\cdots\cdots\cdots\cdots\cdots\cdots\cdots\cdots\cdots$ 110

INDIVIDUALS' SOURCES $\cdots\cdots\cdots\cdots\cdots\cdots\cdots$ 111

PUBLISHED SOURCES $\cdots\cdots\cdots\cdots\cdots\cdots\cdots\cdots$ 113

WEBSITES $\cdots\cdots\cdots\cdots\cdots\cdots\cdots\cdots\cdots\cdots$ 115

INDEX $\cdots\cdots\cdots\cdots\cdots\cdots\cdots\cdots\cdots\cdots$ 116

MAPS:

I   THE FRONT LINE IN FLANDERS DECEMBER 1914 $\cdots\cdots$ 18

II   POSITION OF BRITISH BATTALIONS PLUGSTREET WOOD DECEMBER 1914   23

III ROYAL ENGINEERS' MAP OF PLUGSTREET WOOD AREA DECEMBER 1914 $\cdots$ 28

IV LEUTNANT KURT ZEHMISCH'S MAP OF THE ST. YVES AREA 1914-1915 $\cdots\cdots$ 39

V   LOCATION OF LIEUTENANT BRUCE BAIRNSFATHER'S CHRISTMAS TRUCE .   50

VI DETAILED MAP OF THE PLUGSTREET WOOD AREA DECEMBER 1914 $\cdots\cdots$ 104

THE AUTHORS

Andrew Hamilton (on right): retired in 1989 from teaching History at schools in Hereford and Worcester. He was responsible for the restoration of a watermill to full working order in Warwickshire and managed it as a popular tourist attraction. Since 2008 he has been writing and lecturing on the Great War and started Dene House Publishing in 2009 with the publication of the well-received **Meet at Dawn, Unarmed**, a commentary on his grandfather Robert Hamilton's diary of his experiences with the Royal Warwicks in 1914 and his part in the Christmas Truce at St. Yvon in Belgium.

Alan Reed (on left): retired from full-time teaching in Cheshire in 1996 to concentrate on guiding school and adult groups on the Western Front. He gives

The authors in Plugstreet Wood   *J Kerr*

numerous talks on various aspects of the Great War. His interest was inspired by his father who worked for the Commonwealth War Graves Commission in northern France. A fluent French speaker, his vast knowledge of the battlefield sites of France and Belgium has been invaluable in the research and planning for **Meet at Dawn, Unarmed, Stolen Lives** and **We Good...We No Shoot**.

REVIEWS

MEET AT DAWN, UNARMED: published April 2009

Very many thanks for sending me a copy of your book. It is quite magnificent, all the more so because of the many illustrations synthesised into the text. It is more than usually interesting for a variety of reasons, amongst them the occasional appearances of both B.L. Montgomery and Bruce Bairnsfather, and, of course, for another view of the Christmas Truce... It is a really stupendous effort.
Professor Richard Holmes

An exceptional book that adds so much to our knowledge of the early days of WW1.
Major Tonie and Valmai Holt

It's very different to the other Christmas Truce books...it's a must for the museum shop.
Dominiek Dendooven, In Flanders Fields Museum, Ypres

I think the book is excellent and I'm very pleased to have been involved in a small way.
Mark Warby, Editor of The Old Bill Newsletter about Bruce Bairnsfather

STOLEN LIVES: published May 2014

In *Stolen Lives*, they have raised the standard, for it is a product that puts most recent Great War titles to shame in terms of quality of materials and production, for a similar price. Each story is deeply researched, not only in terms of the individual's biography but the historical context in which they died. Each is profusely illustrated with contemporary and modern photographs. They make for absorbing and sobering reading. It is a great effort that had taken several years in the compilation and a very good read. Recommended.
Chris Baker, 'The Long, Long Trail' (website nominated for an award from the Chartered Institute of Librarians and Information Professionals)

This is the second book by these writers, following on from their excellent account of the Christmas Truce in 'Meet at Dawn, Unarmed' … it is a convenient handbook for battlefield visitors who would like to visit the graves and memorials… the book is produced to very high standards…It's a credit to all who were involved- a beautiful object in its own right and a triumph of self-publishing.
Tom Morgan, 'Hellfire Corner' website

The authors' previous work, *Meet at Dawn, Unarmed* may be known to members of the WFA. I therefore expected another high quality volume and I was not disappointed… I can recommend this book to those having a casual interest in the period but also to more serious students of the conflict.
Stand To! No. 101 September 2014 Western Front Association

It is a beautifully designed book… Stolen Lives is packed with all kinds of fascinating information…
Stratford-upon-Avon Herald, 19 June 2014

It's a beautiful book and so interesting.
Sian Salt, BBC Religion and Ethics, Salford

…as yet I have only read Nellie's story. Yes it made me cry but I think it's wonderful…
Vera Sheard, great niece of Nurse Nellie Spindler, featured as one of the Stolen Lives

Thank you so much for your wonderful book… I hope it does very well as it is such a unique window into the personal sacrifices of so many, and in such an accessible and well-illustrated format… we were very pleased with your piece about Walter, but of course it is much enhanced by your layout and use of photos.
Pat (Finlayson) Justad, great niece of Walter Tull

Meet at Dawn, Unarmed and Stolen Lives by Andrew Hamilton and Alan Reed

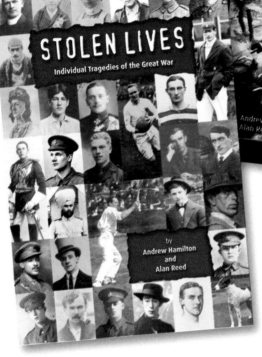

Tonie and Valmai are leading experts on the Western Front and the Plugstreet area. They have written many acclaimed guidebooks and are the authors of the only biography of Bruce Bairnsfather: "In Search of the Better 'Ole A Biography of Captain Bruce Bairnsfather including a Listing of his Works and Collectables".

They are currently engaged in securing recognition for Bruce Bairnsfather's overlooked contribution to the Great War.

FOREWORD

by Tonie and Valmai Holt

By the end of December 1914 British troops had been fighting determinedly in France and Belgium for more than 4 months. By this time the jingoistic, bravado concept that 'the War would be all over by Christmas' had been thoroughly dispelled. The men in the trenches were afflicted by exhaustion, hunger, homesickness, by diseases such as trench foot, by lice and rats, by their comrades being killed and by constant bombardment.

So when Christmas approached, the biblical concept of "Peace on Earth, Goodwill to all Men" temporarily overcame the lust to kill one's enemies. This opportunity to stop the madness was, in the main, first seized by the Germans. The phenomenon became known as 'The Christmas Truce'. It caught the public imagination and does so to this day.

Nowhere was The Truce so well recorded as in the Ploegsteert Sector, just in front of the infamous Wood that came to be known a 'Plugstreet'. Today a small cross erected by the Khaki Chums marks the edge of the field where this historic meeting took place.

No two people are as well qualified as Andrew Hamilton and Alan Reed to examine this extraordinary event.

Alan's father worked with that wonderful organisation, the Commonwealth War Graves Commission, in Northern France. An ex-teacher and now battlefield guide he knows the area intimately.

Andrew, a retired history teacher, discovered that rarest of treasures – a vividly descriptive family diary, that of his grandfather, Captain Robert Hamilton of the 1st Warwicks which covers in detail the progression of the Christmas Truce in 'Plugstreet'.

The authors have shown in their earlier book, based on that diary, *Meet at Dawn Unarmed,* published in 2009, remarkable skill in combining research at forensic level with an overall understanding of what facts and figures really mean. Now they have done that again, in *We Good… We No Shoot*, this time presenting their story in thematic elements – 'Items Exchanged (during the Truce)', 'The Football Matches', 'Official Reactions'… and all of this is woven within diary entries, illustrated with carefully drawn maps, photographs and Bairnsfather's cartoons.

This book is a joy to read and its very fascination hides the fact that this is also a serious academic study of an extraordinary event.

Tonie and Valmai Holt

Prowse Point Cemetery
J Kerr

Christmas Day. **Friday 25**

A DAY, UNIQUE IN THE
WORLD'S HISTORY —
I met their of

The diary of Captain Robert Hamilton   Andrew Hamilton

Astounding, extraordinary, marvellous, strange, unbelievable, unique, memorable and wonderful were some of the words used to describe the Christmas Truce at Plugstreet Wood in Belgium by those who were present.

At this stage of the Great War, the soldiers in the 10th and 11th Infantry Brigades of the British Expeditionary Force were Regulars and Territorials, many of whom had seen service in the Boer War. The former were hardened professionals, trained to defeat and destroy an enemy. It was an iconic moment, when, after four months of some of the most intense and gruelling warfare ever experienced, peace broke out when hundreds of soldiers from both sides met in No Man's Land in an act that contravened one of the fundamental tenets of every military rulebook- that under no circumstances should fraternisation take place with the enemy.

Those that took part in the drama that unfolded in the frozen mud and craters of No Man's Land at Plugstreet Wood, understood the enormity of what they were doing- it was a short moment in their lives that they intended to savour and enjoy to the full and in surprisingly large numbers, soldiers on both sides were keen to commit their memories to paper. We have found a wealth of contemporary accounts by soldiers of the nine battalions who spent the Christmas period in the trenches- the greatest number are the 19 written by soldiers who served with the 1st Battalion of the Royal Warwickshire Regiment and there were two accounts by the Royal Field Artillery officers who happened to be with the Regiment at the time. The London Rifle Brigade was a rich source of material; as it was a Territorial unit, many of the soldiers were from the professions and liable, therefore, to keep diaries and send detailed letters home.

Imagine the scene: on Christmas Eve, the Germans lit candles on Christmas trees along their trenches, star shells (flares) lit up a starry sky, both sets of soldiers sang each other songs and carols, accompanied by an assortment of musical instruments. On Christmas Day and Boxing Day there were gatherings in No Man's Land, halting conversations, exchanges of various 'goodies', photographs were taken and the collecting and burying of each other's dead took place. No wonder it made a lasting impression.

In 2009 Alan Reed and I wrote a commentary on my grandfather, Captain Robert Hamilton's diary account of his experiences with the 1/ Royal Warwicks in *Meet at Dawn, Unarmed*. The story of his war culminated with the truce between the 1/ Royal Warwicks and the 134th Regiment of the Saxon Corps. In the intervening years we have discovered more evidence which makes it one of the best documented of all the armistices that took place along the 425 mile Western Front. We have decided to widen the scope of the research to include the 11th Brigade's five battalions based in the Plugstreet Wood sector.

In the immediate aftermath of the truce, the authorities were keen to play down its existence and censorship was stepped up but to limited effect. Private Alfred Day of the 1/ Royal Warwicks rightly predicted in a letter home that news of the truce was "sure to leak out I think": his letter ended up in the pages of *The Warwick and Warwickshire Advertiser* on 16th January! Other letters from the Front followed in Midlands' newspapers, all of which made it difficult for the authorities to deny what had happened.

The Royal Warwicks' Antelope badge on a headstone
Annette George

Many of the soldiers who had gone to war in August 1914 had fallen for the propaganda that it would be "over by Christmas". Robert Hamilton noted in his diary that there was much discussion as to the probable length of the war: "I gave it to Christmas" he predicted. Little did he realise that the war would come to an end for the 1/Royal Warwicks over Christmas, albeit briefly.

Many of those who fraternised with their adversaries had been engaged in heavy fighting in the most adverse of conditions since late August. The B.E.F.'s 10th and 11th Brigades had been driving the Germans away from Paris, over the rivers Marne and Aisne and then the aim was to prevent them reaching the Channel ports. Early in the campaign it had become clear that a few swift cavalry charges would not seal the end of Kaiser Wilhelm's territorial ambitions; the cavalry had been rendered surplus to requirements and in the First Battle of Ypres in November, cavalry regiments had been reduced to fighting with infantry regiments. The Germans would not be a pushover.

The word 'hell' was often used to describe the gruelling nature of the warfare and the conditions in which it was fought. A chaplain for the 18th Brigade, the Rev. Charles Doudney, described being at the Front as "just simply hell on earth." Referring to the fighting in November, Private William Tapp of the Royal Warwicks recounted he "once or twice had a glimpse of hell". Hamilton described action in the Marne as being "the hell" and that he was sure he looked 50 but felt like a 70 year old. There was plenty more route marching and fighting to come. On 16th November the 1/ Royal Warwicks were in the Armentières area when orders arrived that they were to move on. Hamilton was right to predict "that we are in for some pretty dirty work" and on 21st November "the regiment was moved off to our new trenches near the famous Plugstreet Wood" which became "home" until April 1915 for the two Brigades.

By the end of 1914, the War had already claimed 100,000 British casualties. The slaughter was such that on 7th December Pope Benedict XV pleaded for a halt to the fighting for the celebration of Christmas. He asked "that the guns may fall silent at least upon the night the angels sang." His request was ignored by the authorities of the nations taking part: at least those in the trenches unofficially and "without permission" acted in sympathy with his wishes.

Mobile fighting had now been replaced by attritional trench warfare when a gain of a few hundred yards was considered a major achievement. It was less physically demanding than the earlier campaigns as troops were now confined to trenches. One Royal Warwicks officer, Lieutenant Guy Cave wrote "my uniform is splitting at the seams, this is due to the fact that I have become beastly fat, that is the worst of living this featherbed life" but nonetheless, conditions in the Plugstreet area for British and German soldiers were appalling; stormy, wet weather during the first two weeks of December caused constant flooding in the trenches. Both sides spent more time pumping out their trenches than fighting.

The Christmas Armistice was a short and peaceful interlude in the four years of senseless carnage that followed. After millions of deaths, the War ended. There were few sparks of humanity in that time: the Christmas Truce was described by the celebrated author Sir Arthur Conan Doyle as "one human episode amid all the atrocities which have stained the memory of the war"- his son Kingsley had been seriously wounded during the Battle of the Somme in 1916 and, his defences weakened, he succumbed to Spanish influenza in 1918.

'ell.... Mud to Mufti *by Bruce Bairnsfather*
© *2014 Estate of Barbara Bruce Littlejohn*

Pope Benedict XV

There had been little home leave for those in the B.E.F. of the rank of captain and below. They were worn out and desperate for a break. My grandfather left his home in Devon in July and did not return until January 12th 1915- a long time to be away from his wife and two children. Private Alfred Smith from Warwickshire made the point about the longevity of the campaign but struck a positive note: "We have been in these trenches now for nearly five weeks and what with the rain and mud we could do with a bit of a rest but keep on smiling, and hope to have one someday."

The Christmas Truce was an extraordinary drama- we have tried to let those who took part tell the story, the officers and men in the trenches and their superiors behind the lines. Their words help to explain why and how the truce took place, what happened during it and why it was allowed in certain sectors to continue into the New Year. We also examine why, at a time of overbearing censorship, newspapers were soon awash with first hand reports of what, one hundred years later, has developed into a popular and iconic episode in a long drawn out period of sustained inhumanity.

Andrew Hamilton

Some of the 880,000 ceramic poppies "planted" round the Tower of London in 2014, each commemorating a lost British soldier Andrew Hamilton

ABBREVIATIONS

The following are used in the text:

ADC	Aide-de-camp- a Lieutenant or Captain on a General's personal staff
BEF	British Expeditionary Force
CM	Court Martial
CO	Commanding Officer of a battalion
CQMS	Company Quartermaster Serjeant- in charge of supplies
CWGC	Commonwealth War Graves Commission
DSO	Distinguished Service Order awarded to officers for "distinguished service during active operations against the enemy"
ELR	1/ East Lancashire Regiment
GHQ	General Headquarters
GOC	General Officer Commanding a Brigade, Division, Corps or Army
HR	1/ Hampshire Regiment
LRB	1/5 (City of London) London Regiment- known as The London Rifle Brigade
NCO	Non Commissioned Officer e.g. Corporals and Serjeants
Pte	Private
RAMC	Royal Army Medical Corps
RB	1/ Rifle Brigade
RDF	2/ Royal Dublin Fusiliers
RE	Royal Engineers
RIF	1/ Royal Irish Fusiliers
RFA	Royal Field Artillery
RSM	Regimental Serjeant Major
RWR	1/ Royal Warwickshire Regiment
SH	2/ Seaforth Highlanders
SLI	1/ Somerset Light Infantry

COMPOSITION OF THE BRITISH EXPEDITIONARY FORCE (B.E.F.)
DURING THE GREAT WAR:

Ranks:

Field Marshal	Commander in Chief
General	i/c of an army of approximately 200,000
Lieutenant General	Corps between 30,000 and 75,000
Major General	Division of 20,000
Brigadier General	Brigade of 4,000
Lieutenant Colonel	Battalion of 1,000
Major	Second i/c a battalion
Captain	Company of 250
Lieutenant	Platoon of 60
2nd Lieutenant	Platoon of 60
Other ranks	Serjeants and Corporals
No rank	Privates

Units:

Army	consisting of three to five Corps
Corps	two to five Divisions
Division	three Brigades
Brigade	four Battalions
Battalion	four Companies
Company	four Platoons
Platoon	four Sections of 15

"PLUGSTREET WOOD"

By the end of November the rival armies faced each other in trenches along a 425 mile front which snaked its way from Nieuwpoort on the Belgian coast southwards into France and then eastwards to Verdun and to the Swiss border. The wooded area in and around the village of Ploegsteert would be 'home' for the battalions of the 10th and 11th Brigades and the 134th Infantry Regiment of the XIX (Saxon) Corps. British soldiers, as they did for many places on the Western Front, anglicised the name to "Plugstreet Wood". The wood is situated south of the Ypres Salient, 14 kms from Ypres and about 5 kms from Armentières across the border in France. The wood takes its name from the village of Ploegsteert (Flemish for plough share) to the south west and lies at the southern end of

Plugstreet Wood - from Bullets and Billets *by Bruce Bairnsfather*
© *2014 Estate of Barbara Bruce Littlejohn*

the Messines Ridge. At its furthest extent Plugstreet Wood measures 2.5 kms from west to east and 1 km from north to south. Two small rivers flow west to east, the Douve, which meanders north of the wood and the Warnave to the south. Most of the area is at sea level; higher ground is to the northwest, known to the British as Hill 63 i.e. 63 metres above sea level. It would prove to be a good observation point particularly for the artillery. The main Armentières to Messines (Mesen in Flemish)

road cuts through the western edge of the wood after passing through Ploegsteert. Two hamlets were on the front line- St. Yves (also known as St. Yvon) to the north east and Le Gheer to the south east.

Possibly a Royal Warwicks officer outside a "residence" in St. Yves
South West Heritage Trust

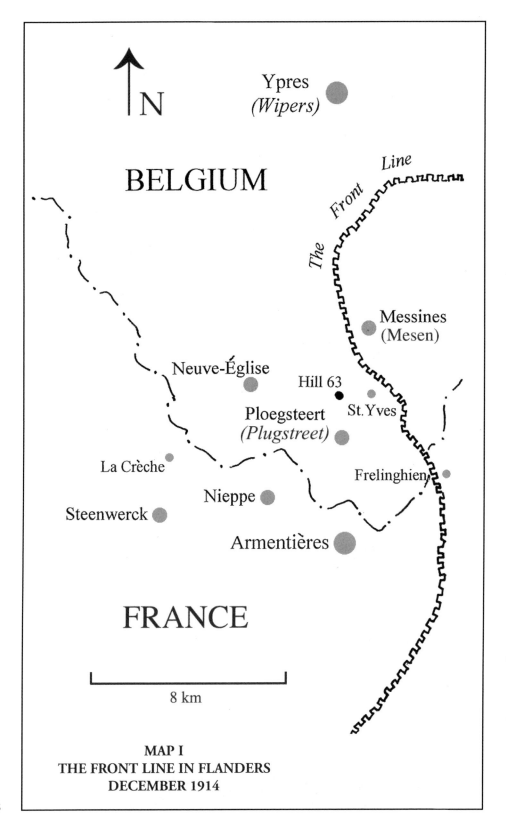

MAP I
THE FRONT LINE IN FLANDERS
DECEMBER 1914

III Corps was commanded by Lieutenant General Sir William Pulteney; within the Corps were two Divisions, one of which, the 4th, was commanded by Major General Henry Wilson. It comprised of three Brigades, the 10th which was holding the line to the north of the wood, the 11th to the east and the 12th which controlled the trenches to the south east.

The 10th Brigade led by Brigadier General Charles Hull, organised their line into a two-battalion front. The 2/ Seaforth Highlanders and the 1/ Royal Irish Fusiliers took it in turns to defend trenches on each side of the Armentières to Messines road. The other battalions to take up their positions to the right in front of St. Yves, were the 1/ Royal Warwicks and the 2/ Royal Dublin Fusiliers. Each battalion would spend four days in the front line trenches and then four days behind the line.

"Plugstreet Hall" was near the southern edge of the wood. Note the Royal Warwicks badge to the left of the door (Map VI = 6D-2)   Claude Verhaeghe

The inside of "Plugstreet Hall"
South West Heritage Trust

19

The 11th Brigade, commanded by Brigadier General Aylmer Hunter-Weston, consisted of the 1/ Rifle Brigade and 1/ Somerset Light Infantry who were entrenched south of St. Yves and, to their right, the 1/ Hampshire and the 1/ East Lancashire at Le Gheer. The 11th Brigade was reinforced by a Territorial unit- the 1/5 (City of London) London Regiment more commonly known as the London Rifle Brigade. The Germans who faced the two British Brigades were the 133rd and 134th Regiments of the XIX (Saxon) Corps and the 6th Jäger Reserve unit.

Plugstreet Wood was described in the Royal Irish Fusiliers Battalion War Diary as "a pleasant enough place when dry or frozen hard, but in the wet it gets feet deep in mud and every trench gets full of water. The soil is clay and the ground is low lying so that the water does not get away and it is difficult to dig more than 2 feet down without coming to water."

Conditions at Plugstreet Wood became the main issue for British and German soldiers- pumping rather than fighting was the order of the day. So bad was the situation that General Sir John French, Commander in Chief of the B.E.F. was moved to write on 10th December: "The heavy rain has almost flooded the trenches, particularly in the neighbourhood of Ploegsteert. The Germans are suffering as much as we are! The men in the trenches say the Saxons call across to them and say they have 'had enough of it'!"

TRENCHES AND MANNING ROUTINES FOR THE 10th AND 11th BRIGADES

10th Brigade:

To the north of Plugstreet Wood, R.J. Kentish of the Royal Irish Fusiliers wrote that his battalion and the Seaforth Highlanders "relieved each other with monotonous regularity, on a basis of four days in and four out." For Serjeant Hugh Wilson (RIF) the trenches were 200 yards apart, a lot further than those of Captain Hamilton's Royal Warwicks which unbelievably were a mere 80 yards!

North east of the Wood, trench duty was shared between the Royal Dublin Fusiliers and the Royal Warwicks, who took their turn without much enthusiasm on Christmas Eve. The routine was the same: "We are having four days in the trenches and four out" according to Private A. Barnett (RWR) who was opposed by Saxons 100 yards away.

11th Brigade:

For Bryan Latham (LRB) "Christmas Day was now approaching and Brigade HQs decided they had sufficient confidence in us that the London Rifle Brigade with their 4 Companies should take over the whole of the front line trenches so that the hard-worked Regiments could spend their Christmas either in support farms or in billets further back." It was unlikely that LRB companies manned the whole of the front line but Brigade commanders were confident enough to let a Territorial unit contribute to front line duty- the Somerset Light Infantry's War Diary on 23rd December records the welcome news that "the London Rifle Brigade are sending a company to each Battalion" (of the 11th Brigade).

A close study of the War Diaries shows that the 11th Brigade operated a different trench routine to the 10th Brigade. As detailed in the 1/Hampshire Battalion War Diary, each battalion had "one company in the firing line, one company in support, one company in reserve at Ploegsteert and one company in billets" in Nieppe, a 5 kilometre march away. In early 1915 the 11th Brigade decided to scrap this system and follow the 10th's which was much easier to manage.

East of the wood, trenches were manned by companies of the Somerset Light Infantry and Rifle Brigade. According to Frederic Coleman, an American volunteer driver attached to the 1st Cavalry Division "The Bosche trenches were only fifty to

Images on left - Plugstreet Wood: clockwise from top left
1. *Planked path and gate in Bunhill Row (Map VI = 5C-1)*   South West Heritage Trust
2. *Soldier on edge of Plugstreet Wood*   Claude Verhaeghe
3. *Soldiers of the S.L.I. in Hunter Avenue (Map VI = 5E and 6E)*   South West Heritage Trust
4. *S.L.I. orderly room*   South West Heritage Trust

Officer outside the H.Q. of the S.L.I. in the wood (Map VI = 5D-1)   *South West Heritage Trust*

seventy yards in front of the Somerset Light Infantry. Their (the Somersets') breastworks about 100 yards behind their front line were for the accommodation of 1st line supports whereas "Touquet Berthe Farm" (Map VI = 7C-1) was occupied by soldiers in reserve." Although in places opposing trenches were very close, a gap of 50 yards was unusual. Corporal Coulson (LRB) wrote about trenches being "at right angles to us which line a hedge of the same field."

Arthur Cook of the Somersets wrote on 18th November that the Somersets were "at the extreme end of Ploegsteert Wood in ditches which were rapidly transferred into trenches. Our trenches take a very curious angle here, just on our left there is a hedge running straight from the wood towards the German lines for about 100 yards, and by the side of it is a trench which then bears sharply left, thus forming a letter Z." (Map VI = 5F) He felt it was very dangerous as it was a "splendid landmark… open to enfilade fire."(i.e. the opponent can fire straight down the length of the trench.) Nonetheless it was not his place to criticise: "It's not for us to grumble and grouse, our duty is to do and obey."

Trenches to the south of the Somerset Light Infantry and the Rifle Brigade were controlled by the East Lancashire and Hampshire Regiments; they were described by Edward Roe (ELR) as being "more or less irregular ditches following twists and angles without any apparent meaning, through turnip fields, across roads, through badly pulverised villages and farmhouses."

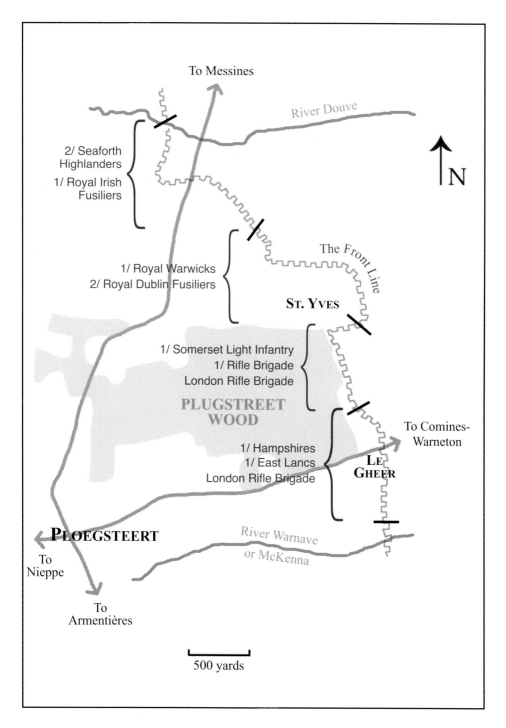

To Messines

River Douve

2/ Seaforth
Highlanders

1/ Royal Irish
Fusiliers

N

The Front Line

1/ Royal Warwicks
2/ Royal Dublin Fusiliers

ST. YVES

1/ Somerset Light Infantry
1/ Rifle Brigade
London Rifle Brigade

PLUGSTREET
WOOD

To Comines-
Warneton

1/ Hampshires
1/ East Lancs
London Rifle Brigade

LE
GHEER

PLOEGSTEERT

River Warnave
or McKenna

To
Nieppe

To
Armentières

500 yards

MAP II
POSITION OF BRITISH BATTALIONS PLUGSTREET WOOD
DECEMBER 1914

December 1914

Lieutenant K.M. Gaunt (RWR) commented in a letter that "it would be too awful to spend a winter where we are." He was right, conditions got worse by the day- the weather in Belgium was particularly poor in December 1914; it was stormy and wet on 1st, 2nd, 3rd and 15th December. Life in the trenches was a constant battle against the elements. The War Diary of the Somerset Light Infantry recorded that a trench was waist high with water and on the following day, tracks in Plugstreet Wood were knee deep in mud "almost everywhere." There are constant references to pumps and the desperate need for them. On 6th December "another force pump was carried up to the trenches with great labour" and on the 7th, "continual pumping and bailing (sic.) does not suffice to keep the water down." On the 9th no pumps were available… "The men were having to stand in water the whole time… most of the dug outs are awash." Hardly ideal for hygiene, the latrines were flooded as well.

Pump 1914 IWM Q53500

Pumps were working overtime. The 1/ Hampshires were pumping water out of their trenches throughout December, and from 20th to 31st "the Company in occupation, having to work day and night pumping and baling out water." The 10th Brigade's diary recorded on 17th December that "new pumps sent up to the trenches last night proved to be a great success."

The battalions in the front line trenches were dependent on assistance from the Royal Engineers. Half a section on 2nd December "took out a pump and arrested the flow of a spring in the Warwicks' trenches at night." The following day works were carried out to pathways in "Muddy Lane" along which some Companies of the 10th Brigade Battalions would march to and from the trenches. They also assisted in building corduroy roads (constructed with logs or planks) but the Royal Engineers spent Christmas Eve mending pumps and preparing barbed wire and posts.

Mud or Muddy Lane with the Wood in the background (Map VI = 5B and 4C) Andrew Hamilton

Lieutenant Guy Cave (RWR) described the weather as "our other enemy" and that it was "worse than ever. One sleeps in water and to look at, you would hardly believe that the men from head to foot in mud as they are, are the same khaki-clad people you know." Private Walter Cooke (RWR) wrote home praying for freezing weather: "… for we have had plenty of wet since I have been here. At times we have had the water above our knees all night in the trenches." The mud was appalling and the extent of it overlooked- we tend to associate mud with Passchendaele in 1917. Corporal Arthur Cook (SLI) recorded that in places mud was "two and three feet deep, and if a man was unlucky enough to slip in it in the dark, he had little chance of struggling out. I fear we lost several men in this way." Private A. Barnett (RWR) was finding that "life in the trenches with the wet weather was most trying."

Corduroy road in wood
South West Heritage Trust

In his *Bullets and Billets*, Bruce Bairnsfather recalled that he was "covered with mud from head to foot, cold as a fish, and reclining in about a foot of water in such a position as to ruin all my cigarettes and matches." In an article entitled *One Night in Flanders*, he wrote of how "Tommy", in the guise of his greatest creation "Old Bill", had to endure the most dreadful of conditions: "My dear Old Bill was there… he seemed too full to speak, and whenever he did, his verbiage was of a kind that should be heard in the Gentlemen's Smoking Room only… Old Bill and his companions endured the atrocious conditions with almost Oriental indifference, but found considerable relief in bad and unprintable language."

Owing to an excess of water in the 1/ Somerset Light Infantry's trenches, Corporal Cook recorded that a barricade was built behind a flooded trench but he did not like the position: "We have no cover from shells and not much cover from bullets."

Frederic Coleman describes the horrendous conditions: "A jaunt in Ploegsteert Wood was a muddy experience… All about were broken and splintered branches and tree trunks- a weird place… The Tommies in the trench line were knee-deep in water. Men passed plastered in mud. An officer told me a Tommy's overcoat, weighed in the village, had tipped the scale at 45 pounds." (20 kilos)

The author Henry Williamson (who in 1927 wrote *Tarka the Otter*) of the London Rifle Brigade, a Territorial unit, complained over Christmas that he had suffered "an awful time with swollen feet… my toes are frostbitten now." He and the majority of those at the Front, took matters in their stride: "But it is all in a day's work, as is working all night at digging etc. and sleeping in wet and mud…"

Lieutenant Le Mare (RIF) in mud, winter 1914/15
Royal Irish Fusiliers Museum, Armagh

The views of two of the Corps Commanders differ on how "Tommy" was coping. General Sir Horace Smith-Dorrien's retrospective appraisal was how "wonderful" it was the way difficulties were overcome, "but what looms largest in my wonder is the heroism and dogged cheerfulness of the troops under awful conditions in spite of the heavy daily toil." General Sir Douglas Haig, on the other hand, pointed out to King George V and the Prince of Wales when he met them for dinner on 4th December that British troops were not all by nature brave and great efforts had to be made by commanders to keep up the morale of their men.

The 134th Saxons suffered as much if not more than their British counterparts as their trenches were nearer the river Douve which flooded on several occasions during the month. The 2/ Royal Dublin Fusiliers reported seeing Germans baling out their trenches on 5th December. The situation had become so critical that according to the 1/ Royal Warwicks' War Diary: "The Dublin Fusiliers enquire whether an armistice could be arranged for both sides to bail (sic) out their trenches." It is interesting, therefore, to note that three weeks before the Christmas Truce, there was already talk, on practical grounds, of a ceasefire.

Captain Hamilton (RWR) described the trenches as "deplorable" and Private William Tapp (RWR) maintained amusingly that "it will take boats to relieve us"! Humour in adversity was a way of lifting the gloom. On 11th December, Hamilton entered in his diary: "It rained all night and the whole of today. When I went round the sentries I found them quite resigned to another flood. They were amused. One Private Carter said 'it will lay the dust, sir, won't it?' at which I laughed heartily and so did they. But poor fellows they were on their last legs for this trench trip. Cave had to spend the day and night in my dug out as his was flooded." Lieutenant Cave commented in a letter that "we are having a real bad time of it with the weather." Arthur Cook (SLI) was also unimpressed with life in the trenches: "I sat down in a little dug out about large enough for a decent single rat, changed my socks, had my tot of rum and went to sleep 'just as I was', with plenty of fleas."

An Army does, after all, march on its stomach… Basil Kentish, nephew of Brigadier-General R.J. Kentish, writes that when his uncle was a Major in the Royal Irish Fusiliers he was adamant that the flooded trenches should not lower meal standards: "With the help of Fortnum and Mason hampers, reinforced by a daily bottle of champagne which came up for him mysteriously from the back areas and aided or abetted by his cook, Private Atter, he had established quite a notable Company Mess."

The kilt-wearing Seaforth Highlanders were finding the cold a trial when there was a brief return to snow and frost over Christmas. On 28th December Jim Davie thanked his wife Ciss for sending some stockings which would cover his knees although he was not sure if he would be allowed to wear them! "…We use anything to keep ourselves warm, some have drawers others long stockings and all of us boots and puttees, I can assure you we don't look the peaceful Highlanders you see at home…"

At least the severity of the conditions facing Tommy in the trenches was recognised by High Command; Field Marshal Sir John French understood that "the rain, the cold and the awful holding ground seemed to damp down every energy".

Stoical though they were, the conditions did get the better of some soldiers- their misery was such that according to Serjeant Hugh Wilson (RIF) "it was not uncommon to catch the sentries standing on the parapet, hoping to get shot they felt that miserable." In a note from the 11th Brigade to the 4th Division, detailing the casualties for 29th December, it was recorded that the Hampshires had "one man admitted to hospital on 28th December with a self-inflicted wound."

German snipers and artillery were a constant danger. Private William Setchfield from Newark in Nottinghamshire, was a regular who had been with the Royal Warwicks for seven years: "The German shells keep bursting over us and deadly artillery they are."

Enemy shell and rifle fire were also a threat to those not far behind the front line in Le Gheer village, particularly for the locals. Private Edward Roe (ELR) tells of how the owners of *estaminets* (cafés) and quite a few villagers were managing to hold on to their homes although it was "barely out of rifle range and is shelled every day. It is quite common to see children playing in the village streets whilst the village is being shelled. Four of five of us were often in an estaminet having a drink of beer (of course we're not supposed to be there, but we do a lot of things we're not supposed to do and so do our superiors) and a shell would arrive in the house next door. The proprietor would grab two kids and make a dive for the cellar followed by his better half exclaiming 'Souvenir Allemands, Souvenir Allemands!' We would all look at each other and remark 'Oh Jerry's got his 'rag out' again.'"

Anyone working within range of enemy artillery was subject to a random death. Ration parties bringing food to the forward trenches at night were at risk; Private Roe described how they had to "go back almost a mile over shell and machine-gun swept roads. One third of the party invariably get 'seen off' each night. You come across a biscuit box on the road; Tom or Bill or Dick is 'panned out' beside it… Two more mounds and two more wooden crosses adorn the turnip field in the rear of our trenches next morning and so the lottery of death goes on."

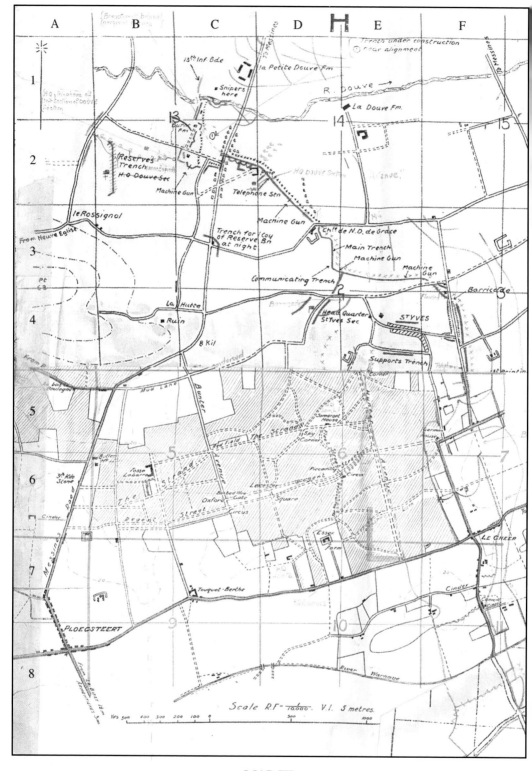

MAP III
ROYAL ENGINEERS' MAP OF PLUGSTREET WOOD AREA
DECEMBER 1914

An interesting memorandum was sent on 4th December from G. Forestier-Walker, on behalf of General Smith-Dorrien, commander of II Corps, concerning general tactical policy which the GOC II Corps "wishes to be adopted for the present… Friendly intercourse with the enemy, unofficial armistices (e.g. 'we won't fire if you don't' etc.) and the exchange of tobacco and other comforts, however tempting and occasionally amusing they may be, are absolutely prohibited." Smith-Dorrien had been made aware of the dangers of over familiarity between the lines from a surprisingly early stage. In his memoirs he told of how on the morning of 29th September, the Germans "with the greatest respect for the accuracy of British fire, put up a dummy figure above one of the trenches, at which our men promptly began to shoot, when out of the trench appeared a spade, indicating against the figure the position of each of its hits and yet they say the Germans have no sense of humour." At least Smith-Dorrien admitted that evidence for it was flimsy but was amused by a story relayed to him that "our soldiers had been shouting to the Germans opposite to come out, without result, and a subaltern stood up in his trench and shouted 'Waiter', and at once a dozen heads appeared, shouting 'Coming sir!'" There is much evidence to show that many Germans were employed in English restaurants and hotels before 1914.

It can be demonstrated that the fraternisations over Christmas and the New Year had their roots in incidents in the run up to Christmas. The Royal Dublin Fusiliers'

Map III opposite   National Archives WO95/ 1440

The regular series of printed British trench maps began to appear in July 1915. Previously 'tactical' maps were lithographed in small numbers by G.H.Q. Printing Company of the Royal Engineers and are now quite rare. It is therefore with a sense of surprise and excitement that we discovered in the National Archives such a map for Plugstreet Wood. It was hidden away in the back cover of the 4th Division file. Dr. Peter Chasseaud, the expert on trench maps, identified it as map 296 from the 1st Printing Company of the Royal Engineers on a 1:10,000 scale, printed in December 1914 before Christmas. The front line defended by the Battalions of the 10th Brigade are clearly shown in brown, north and north east of the wood. The German line is marked in blue. In square 1E is La Douve Farm known to the Germans as Wasserburg (Map IV on page 39). The H.Q. for the Seaforth Highlanders and Royal Irish Rifles is in 2D. The Royal Warwicks and Royal Dublin Fusiliers are in 4D. Some of the Royal Warwicks and Royal Dublin Fusiliers would have used Mud (Muddy) Lane to march to their line, 5B to 4D. In the wood the majority of the names given to paths and other places have a London connection which reflect the humour of the men of the London Rifle Brigade and acted as a reminder for them of home. The Strand is in 6C and in 6D can be found Leicester Square and Piccadilly Circus. Hunter Avenue is in squares 5E and 6E; it was a support line with breastworks about 250 yards behind the 11th Brigade's front line. German House, one of the objectives of the attack on 19th December is in 5F.

suggestion of an armistice was not the only example of increasing "friendliness" between the adversaries. In the period from 16th to 20th December when the 1/ Royal Warwicks were manning the trenches, Private William Tapp of 'C' Company recalled that the Saxons "put a target for us to shoot at, so we did the same and signalled to each other a hit or a miss." Corporal Cook (SLI) maintained that the trenches were so close, in one place just 100 yards, and "every time we snipe at them, they signal with a shovel whether it's a hit or a miss. It's a grim kind of humour."

On 17th December Cook reported that "there has been a lot of shouting in the German lines tonight. I do not know if it is to try and draw our fire, if so, they have not succeeded yet."

The 10th Brigade War Diary acknowledged on Tuesday 22nd December that "in front of the 2/ Royal Dublin Fusiliers' centre Company, a notice was put up by the enemy stating that prisoners would be kindly treated. A suitable reply will be put up by the 2/ Royal Dublin Fusiliers tonight."

Elsewhere "friendliness" was in the air. The 12th Brigade based near the Frelinghien area in France reported the situation up to 7 p.m. on 10th December: "The Germans when kindly offered some rum by our men, declined it saying they themselves drank nothing but champagne in the trenches. The exchange of drinks has not yet been arranged"! The superior drink available in the German trenches was a happy consequence of their progress through Belgium and France in the early weeks of the War.

Effect of German shelling on a street in St. Yves   South West Heritage Trust

In December sniper fire and shelling were the main dangers for both sides in the Plugstreet Wood area. Serjeant Hugh Wilson (RIF) noted that "added to the near constant bombardment from enemy guns was the ever-present danger from snipers." The 1/ Hampshires War Diary noted that from 1st to 18th December there was practically "no fighting."

The situation changed dramatically on 19th December when a major operation was carried out by the 1/ Somerset Light Infantry, 1/ Hants and 1/ Rifle Brigade of the 11th Brigade, on German trenches east of the Wood. The 1/Royal Warwicks provided covering fire with Bruce Bairnsfather being involved as the machine-gun officer.

"The object of the attack by the 11th Infantry Brigade in front of Ploegsteert Wood" according to Colonel Bates in his *Short History of the London Rifle Brigade* was "to clear its edges, including German House, and, if possible, establish a line in front of an area later known as "The Birdcage". The Somerset Light Infantry and the Rifle Brigade attacked with the London Rifle Brigade in support. The weather could not have been worse and the ground was impossible. The result was that the wood was cleared and German House remained in No Man's Land." The Rifle Brigade took "German House" and reached "Second House" (Map VI = 5F-3) from which they were forced to withdraw. "The mud made rifles impossible to fire." Three officers in the Rifle Brigade were killed (including Captain the Hon. Richard George Morgan-Grenville aged 27 and 34 year old Captain the Hon. Reginald Prittie- both were buried in Rifle House Cemetery) as well as 23 other ranks: 42 other ranks were wounded. 'B' Company of the Somersets attacked "The Birdcage" at 2.30 p.m. the enemy being 120 yards away. As they left this trench, Private Roe (ELR), who was not involved, recalled that "they were greeted by an inferno of shrapnel, rifle and machine-gun fire". Casualties increased as some British shells fell short and exploded amongst the attackers. Roe remembered that "the Germans kept on yelling from behind their formidable array of barbed wire and machine guns, 'Come on the 'Sets! Come on the 'Sets!'"

The Somersets lost five officers including 39 year old Captain Charles Maud D.S.O., Captain Orr who was 34 and Captain Bradshaw together with 27 other ranks; 52 were wounded and 30 were recorded as missing. According to the Regimental History, the survivors were "found in a house- Somersets in one room, German troops in another." Frank Wrentmore who survived the attack wrote: "We had a good skirmish on December 19th when we were successful in taking the trenches of the Germans opposed to us. We, however, had to retire from them because they were full of water."

The Hampshires assisted in the attack and sustained some casualties- the Battalion's acting CO Major George Parker, aged 44, and 15 other ranks were killed and 25 wounded. Parker was buried in Ploegsteert Churchyard. Henry Williamson (LRB) spoke of his terror when waiting in the reserve trenches and one of his abiding memories was of a wounded soldier being taken through the wood, singing "Oh for the wings of a dove". Private Edward Roe (ELR) was aware when night fell that "parties of volunteers and stretcher-bearers carried the wounded in all through the night." He believed that the stretcher-bearers of the London Rifle Brigade deserved special mention. In an act that he felt underlined the inherent goodness of those fighting, Roe mentions a selfless and humane action when "one brave German carried a badly wounded Somerset in on his back. He was thanked and granted a safe passage back to his own lines."

The original grave of 39 year old Captain Charles Maud D.S.O. of the S.L.I. in the wood, now Ploegsteert Wood Military Cemetery (Map VI = 5D-1) South West Heritage Trust

Corporal Arthur Cook's description of the attack is of interest: some of the Royal Artillery's shells, he believed, were bursting over the Royal Warwicks trenches to the left of the Somersets. This was vigorously denied by Brigade Head Quarters. In the 4th Division War Diary it was recorded that "the 10th Brigade report our shells falling in the Warwicks. It was explained to them they could only be German shells."

The noise was deafening, no one could hear themselves speak.

The attack started at 2.30 p.m.- Cook emphasises the terrible conditions, "the ground was so heavy, men could scarcely walk let alone run" which made progress very slow. The men of 'B' Company were carrying mats, described in the Somerset Light Infantry's War Diary as "wire mattresses made out of rabbit wire stuffed with straw" to aid them in scaling the Germans' barbed wire entanglements. 16th and 17th December had been spent practising their use but carrying a mat, their weapons and supplies must have made it virtually impossible to progress quickly through the mud… Cook noticed that "our 6 inch shells were falling horribly short, one fell right in a section of our men killing them all… That alone is a sad story to relate" he concluded.

The attacks floundered about 20 yards short of the front line trenches but the Germans had retired from them to stronger ones further back. Cook is scathing in his criticism of the operation: "It was a bad day's work for the Somersets, there were very heavy casualties and nothing in reward for it… precious lives were thrown away in an attempt to take a few yards of ground, not worth the death of one British Tommy… It was an awful day and I was very glad when it was over, the groans of the wounded were terrible especially at night." He reiterated that it was "an awful day and very disastrous to the regiment. The odds were dead against us but in spite of that, a very brave attempt had been made only to end in failure and saddest of all the loss of valuable lives." The Battalion War Diary maintained that 80 yards were gained "which was our objective."

In contrast to Cook's account, Major Sutton, the Somerset Light Infantry's Commanding Officer, did not see the action in the same light: "From the Battalion's point of view the only effects of the action were of a sentimental nature, firstly pride at the gallant behaviour of the attacking companies who advanced without hesitation against an unshaken line of well-armed defenders, and secondly, grief at the loss of so many well-loved comrades"- particularly, one could add, at the hands of their own artillery's fire…

Leutnant Kurt Zehmisch of the 134th Saxon Regiment discovered that when the "murderous" gunfire took place, the English had tried to attack the position of the '106': "The English managed to advance up to the wire defences but then had to retreat with bloody heads. They had about 600 dead and wounded" a claim which was wildly wide of the mark. Kurt's son Rudolph communicated with us in 2009 and asked the question as to "whether this was so necessary so close to Christmas?" One can assume that British High Command must have hoped that Christmas could be spent celebrating

Leutnant Kurt Zehmisch seated, photographed in a front line trench in March 1915 "by my head are fire slits"
In Flanders Fields Museum, Ypres

a major breakthrough, despite the appalling conditions under foot. In the event, it was the kind of ill-thought out operation so ridiculed in the 1960s and 1970s.

There was little activity after the attack on 19th December; on 23rd December there was a fall of snow; both sides were winding down to the Christmas period and a ceasefire was probably the best that those due for a spell in the trenches could have hoped for…

Kurt Zehmisch
In Flanders Fields Museum, Ypres

After the attack on 19th December, a warning was issued from 4th Division H.Q.: "It is thought possible that the enemy may be contemplating an attack during Christmas and New Year and special vigilance will be maintained during these periods." How wrong they were! Christmas was approaching and the German commanders, unlike their British counterparts, saw no point in ordering their men over the top with little chance of taking any ground.

CHRISTMAS EVE

On 23rd December, the 2/ Seaforth Highlanders left their billets in La Crèche over the border in France and relieved the 1/ Royal Irish Fusiliers.

At 7.40 p.m. on 24th December, the 10th and 11th Brigades were sent a memorandum from the 4th Division's G.H.Q. impressing the need for "vigilance during Christmas and New Year's days."

On Christmas Eve, the 1/ Royal Warwicks' four day stint in the trenches was due to start early in the evening with relief of the Royal Dublin Fusiliers, a prospect that filled them all with doom and gloom. At least the mail had arrived; millions of cards and parcels were delivered to and from the Front within sometimes just two days, an amazing feat of organisation helped by the fact that the B.E.F. was no longer on the move. Private Walter Cooke (RWR) took his parcels with him to the trenches, Serjeant Barrs of the Cyclist Corps, (attached to the 4th Division), was delighted to receive newspapers only two days old and Lieutenant Frank Black (RWR) had no

In and Out (I)

That last half-hour before "going in" to the same trenches for the 200th time

Officers of the Royal Warwicks filled with doom and gloom before relieving the Royal Dublin Fusiliers on Christmas Eve © 2014 Estate of Barbara Bruce Littlejohn

less than 12 letters to read. Captain Hamilton chose to go for a ride but "the mud and slush made it most unenjoyable."

The 2/ Royal Dublin Fusiliers reported "a quiet day" but one man was wounded and two men were killed, Private T. Delany and Private Patrick McCarthy, aged 26. Both were buried in Prowse Point

Cemetery. The artillery behind the lines shelled the Germans at La Petite Douve (Map VI = 1C) but "no movement of Germans was observed."

On being relieved by the Seaforth Highlanders at 6.30 p.m. on 23rd December, the 1/ Royal Irish Fusiliers started their preparations for Christmas and as a special treat, all in the Battalion were issued with long-sleeved goatskin waistcoats. Private

Roe (ELR) was lukewarm about the issue of "sheep or rabbit skin coats... Christ, are we not carrying enough already?" he moaned: "We christen them 'louse traps'. Some of them are floating about the trenches now. They are alright for people at the base… but it is a waste of public money issuing them out to men in the trenches."

In and Out (II)

That first half-hour after "coming out" of those same trenches

The same officers on their return have broken into their Fortnum and Mason hamper. Captain Hamilton is portrayed by Bairnsfather, entertaining them with a German concertina he found in an empty trench
© 2014 Estate of Barbara Bruce Littlejohn

It was with heavy hearts that 'A' Company of the 1/ Royal Warwicks set off for the trenches marching from La Crèche via Mud Lane (Map VI = 5B to 4D) to St. Yves "a little sad at spending Christmas day in them." Captain Robert Hamilton's description is one of the most vivid and detailed of all the accounts: "Crossing the well-worn danger zone to our consternation not a shot was fired at us. The Dubs told us as we relieved them that the germans wanted to talk to us. When we were settled down, we heard them shouting, 'Are you the Warwicks?' To which our men replied 'Come and see'. They said 'You come half way, and we will come half way, and bring you some cigars'. This went on for some time, when Pte. Gregory, Double Ginger, my late servant came and asked if he might go out half way. I said 'Yes, at your own risk'. Private Gregory stepped over the parapet, and got half way, and was heard saying, 'Well here I am, where are you?'

Royal Warwicks' trench   Royal Regiment of Fusiliers Museum (Royal Warwickshire)

'Come half way' they said so on went Gregory, until he came upon two unarmed germans, and one fully armed, lying down just behind, with his rifle pointed at him, typically german. Gregory was unarmed and alone. Typically British. He got

35

his cigar and spun them some magnificent yarns about the strength of his company, which amused us all very much when he told us later. They wanted me to meet their officer, and after a great deal of shouting across, I said I would meet him at dawn, unarmed." Hamilton refused to write the word "German" with a capital letter…

Private Gregory had been Hamilton's batman or officer's servant. He had been sacked on 4th December because "he cannot make tea or anything approaching it." Maybe he was keen to prove a point and impress his officer by offering to go into No Man's Land. At least his spin-doctoring about the strength of his Company was more impressive than his tea-making! Hamilton's decision to allow Gregory to venture out towards the enemy was a brave one given what could have happened to his ex-batman or foolhardy for his own career prospects as it was in contravention of orders similar to those issued by General Smith-Dorrien on 4th December to II Corps. (Hamilton was in III Corps.) An unnamed member of the Rifle Brigade commented in a letter to *The Times* about a similar action by two officers to his right, (probably the Hampshires): "It was an awfully stupid thing to do as it might easily have had different results."

Hamilton's account tallies with that of Lieutenant Black (RWR): "One of our men went out unarmed and met two Germans halfway between our trenches and amid cheers from both lines they lit each other's cigarettes." Serjeant J. Philpotts' (RWR) recollection was that "our line was only 70 yards from the Germans with turnips growing in between the barbed wire." Bairnsfather also mentioned the same root crop.

Next to Hamilton's 'A' Company were 'C' Company- a Serjeant Rea met two Germans, exchanged gifts with them and lit some cigarettes. The precise location of their meeting (Map VI = 3E-1) was "near the remnants of a hedge and ditch which ran out at right angles from our trenches to the Germans." This description by Bruce Bairnsfather accords with Private Tapp's (quoted in its original form): "We have got settled now, it is about 7 pm and one of the Ger's who can speak Eng is shouting over to us to go over, we shout back 'Come half way' it is agreed on, our sergeant goes out their man takes a lot of coaxing but comes at the finish and we find they have sent two we can hear them talking quite plain they exchange cigarettes and the German shouts to wish us Merry Xmas we wait for the Sergeant's return, he gets back and tells us they are not going to fire tonight and not tomorrow if we don't, they have got lights all along their trench and also a Xmas tree lit up they are singing so we give them one, it is funny to hear us talk to one another our stretcher bearers have nothing to do no wounded to carry tonight, so they have all come from headquarters and are going round carol singing, they sing several in our
trench before going, the Ger's give them a cheer for singing…"

Leutnant Kurt Zehmisch's 'A' section held a service at 5.00 p.m. in a half-ruined sugar factory. He tells of a priest giving a sermon about the birth of Christ and the Holy Night after which they sang "Stille Nacht". Candles on Christmas trees flickered as the priest told them they were from a great and proud nation. After singing "O Happy, O Blessed" and "Deutschland, Deutschland über alles", the Saxons made their way to their trenches. Zehmisch ordered his men not to shoot if it could be avoided. He and Private Möckel, who had spent several years in England, called out in English which led to a merry exchange with the Royal Warwicks' 'C' Company: "We wanted to meet halfway between our positions, which were about 100 metres apart and exchange cigars and cigarettes. Möckel and Private Huss made their way through the barbed wire and were approached bit by bit from the other side by two Englishmen in a natural field ditch. After some few minutes of calling to each other and ensuring they had no weapons and no shots would be fired, an Englishman emerged from the ditch and held up his hands- in one he held a cap full of English cigarettes and tobacco. The Englishman now came up to our two men and wished them a merry Christmas and his greeting was heartily returned. Both sides applauded and shouted 'Bravo' enthusiastically. They now swapped cigars and cigarettes, lit them and engaged in conversation. The Englishman called over 'I wish you a Merry Christmas and a Happy New Year'." Zehmisch thanked him very much and he wished him the same: "The Englishman shouted out a promise not to shoot today and tomorrow." The two parties said their farewells and returned to the trenches. More candles were lit on fir trees along the kilometre of German trench: "The English expressed their joy at this and clapped their hands. All manner of Christmas songs and songs of the homeland were sung and from the village the strains of the band playing Christmas carols could be heard through the star-lit night." Zehmisch went through the barbed wire entanglement for 50 metres with Private Huss and spoke with the English. Overcome with excitement he remained awake all night- it was, he concluded, "a wonderful if rather cold night".

The 2/ Seaforth Highlanders were to the left of the Royal Warwicks and there are mixed reports about the level of their involvement over the Christmas and New Year period. Jim Davie's letter to his wife Ciss, is clear that "we had an extraordinary Christmas Eve, the Germans who hold Xmas in great style started giving us songs and shouting little bits in English and of course we retaliated." According to the Seaforths' Battalion War Diary, the Germans were "making great noise last night. Singing and shouting. Some came towards our line and called for our men to go over to them and two or three men went over and spoke to them and got quite close to their trenches and they reported the farm south of La Douve was occupied with considerable numbers of Germans round it and a number were singing east of Avenue and some are reported to have been wearing pickelhaubes, mostly caps or woollen helmets and some khaki-covered shakos and regimental numbers on shoulders thought to be 10 and 28."

A similar scenario occurred to the right further down the line as told by Private B. Hutchings of the 11th Brigade's 1/ Hampshires: "Our Company officer's name was Captain Unwin. The Saxons were beckoning with their hands for us to go over to their trench. But we shouted over that we would meet them half way so Captain Unwin asked

Leutnant Zehmisch's photo of the ruin of La Douve Farm known to the Germans as Wasserburg (Map VI = 1E-1) In Flanders Fields Museum, Ypres

for a volunteer. I happened to be standing by the side of him at the time and it fell to my lot to go over and meet one of the Saxons…"

The 1/ Rifle Brigade to the right of the Somersets were soon aware of German initiatives to encourage a ceasefire. The Wray brothers (LRB) heard a voice from a German trench: "We good… we no shoot" and for them "was born an unofficial armistice." One member of the Brigade recalled that the Germans started singing and lighting candles about 7.30 and one of them challenged any one of us to go across for a bottle of wine. One of our fellows accepted the challenge; that started the ball rolling…"

Lance Corporal Coulson (LRB) reckoned that when it got dark as they were waiting to be relieved from duty in the advance trenches, "singing and shouting was heard coming from the other trenches at right angles to us which line a hedge of the same field. We all sang every song we could think of, a bonfire was lit and everyone walked about as though it were a picnic. After we were relieved and got back to the breastworks (a breast-high fortification constructed from logs, sandbags and mud) behind the firing-lines, we could hear the German band playing 'Old Folks at Home', 'God save the King' and 'Onward Christian Soldiers'." Lance Corporal J.S. Calder of the same Brigade mentions that soldiers from both sides were walking around bonfires.

Map IV opposite   *In Flanders Fields Museum*

The map by Leutnant Kurt Zehmisch of the area north of the Wood during the winter of 1914-1915 shows clearly the German trenches in blue and the British line in red. It is interesting to note the different names given to the same positions by the opposing troops- for full details see the notes for Map VI on page 105

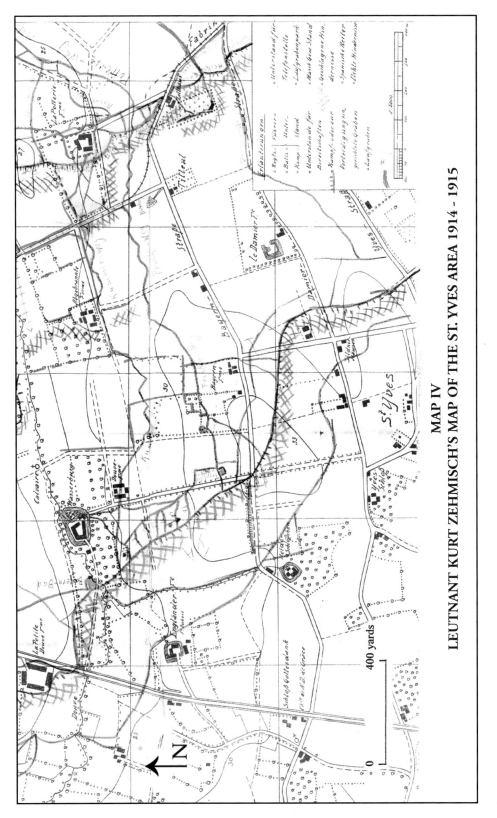

MAP IV

LEUTNANT KURT ZEHMISCH'S MAP OF THE ST. YVES AREA 1914 - 1915

The account of Private Edward Roe (ELR) is the only one to mention that when both sides sang carols their happy tones were "accompanied by uncalled-for bursts of machine-gun and rifle-fire." He mentioned how Old Jim was "seen off" just after 11 p.m. by a stray bullet: "What a Christmas for his wife and kiddies. Has mankind forgotten the Shepherds, the Magi, and the Child that was born in the manger because there was no room for him in the inns of Bethlehem?" It would appear that "Jim" must be Private J.P. Finnigan (ELR) who was buried in the London Rifle Brigade Cemetery- the date is recorded by the CWGC as 25th December 1914.

Roe stood on the fire-step, gazing into No Man's Land "with the point of a spare bayonet underneath my chin in case I might doze." (Falling asleep on duty could entail, at worst, execution. Field Marshal French's diary entry for 12th December notes that "there have been some bad cases of men 'sleeping on post' lately and I much fear an example may soon have to be made.'") I prayed to God, if there was a God, in his infinite goodness and mercy to end this slaughter and misery and bring peace and goodwill to all mankind."

All was not sweetness and light on Christmas Eve… Lance Corporal Coulson (LRB) recounted how after his platoon was relieved by his old friends in No. 6 platoon, when they reached the breastworks "they wanted two volunteers to go with two stretcher-bearers to bring in a poor chap in No. 7 platoon who was sniped at 2.30 just an hour or so before the truce. I am not vengeful but I was jolly glad to hear that a Somerset chap waited for the sniper and got him…" He was referring to a popular member of the unit, a fine baritone singer, 21 year old Rifleman Arthur Bassingham who was shot through the head and is buried in Ploegsteert Wood Military Cemetery.

The events that took place on Christmas Eve at St. Yves and other areas along the Western Front were a spontaneous reaction to a number of factors. All soldiers were jaded after weeks of battling with the elements and the mud. Many comrades had been sniped or killed by shellfire- bodies were still rotting in No Man's Land. They were tired, homesick and in need of a break. It was no surprise that when, in the main, other ranks on both sides shouted out Christmas greetings and invitations to meet, senior officers in the trenches should give, without the agreement of their superiors who were safely behind the lines celebrating, the go-ahead for what would prove to be a momentous and memorable event.

CAROLS, CONCERTINAS AND MOUTH ORGANS ON CHRISTMAS EVE

Once the 134th Saxon Regiment began to sing carols and songs, it was accepted as a gesture of peace and goodwill by the British. Rifleman G. Williams (LRB) who was east of the wood, remembered the Germans singing "The First Nowell", "O Tannenbaum", and "O Come All Ye Faithful". He appreciated the irony of the scenario: "I thought this an extraordinary thing- two nations both singing the same carol in the middle of a war."

A regimental band was brought up opposite the Somerset Light Infantry according to the War Diary, and, at about 2 o'clock in the morning, the London Rifle Brigade heard the German band come out of the trenches and play carols which according to Lance Corporal Calder was "wonderful to hear".

Private Dixon (RWR) heard at 2.00 a.m. on Christmas morning a German band playing "very touchingly" a couple of German tunes and then "Home Sweet Home". They then played "God Save the King" and not surprisingly "we all cheered". Private Layton (RWR) recalled that singing went on for most of the night: "We would sing a song or a carol first and they would sing one and I tell you they can harmonise all right." The Germans had a band of concertinas in the trenches which for Private Walter Cooke (RWR) "sounded great- much better than hearing shells whistle overhead."

A Somerset Light Infantry Private remembered the Germans singing a lot: "But the best was to come. A German bloke had a cornet, and he could play it grand. He just made it talk."

Lieutenant Bruce Bairnsfather (RWR) wrote that "the arrival of sundry mouth organs in the post had enabled some of our mouth organ specialists to get under way." They accompanied a rendering of "Tipperary", a marching song thought to have emanated from the music hall entertainer Jack Judge of Oldbury in the Black Country or from Harry Williams of Temple Balsall who sang it in the Tipperary pub there.

Serjeant J. Philpotts (RWR) was precise: "At exactly midnight a good male voice choir in the enemy line struck up 'Mid Pleasures and Palaces we may roam' and sang verses and chorus of 'Home Sweet Home' in good English." In a *History of the Great War* based on official documents, reference is made to both sides during the evening singing "Auld Lang Syne".

That Evening Star-shell.

"Oh, star of eve, whose tender beam
Falls on my spirit's troubled dream."

—*Wolfram's Aria in "Tannhäuser."*

Private Charlie Pratt (RWR) wrote that star shells "lit up the place lovely and then for the first time we saw friend and foe." Bruce Bairnsfather's cartoon shows a Bert or Alf who has been caught in the spotlight with a rum jar © 2014 Estate of Barbara Bruce Littlejohn

A letter by Private John Mackay (SH) was published in *The Ayr Advertiser* on 28th January 1915: "I was on sentry duty just as Christmas Day arrived and I must confess that it was indeed beautiful to hear the Germans singing carols and their national anthem. We too were all singing and cheering at the pitch of our voices; it was just like being at home." It was an all-night party for at four o'clock in the morning, Mackay wrote that the Germans struck up again with four or five musical instruments: "during all the time the music was being wafted through the air you could hear a pin fall."

Private Pentelow (RB) told his sister about the singing of carols and songs- the Germans would "chime in" and cheer and entertained them with a few instruments. Their rendering of 'Home, Sweet Home' "was very good and anyone who had a home must have thought of it." They followed this with the British national anthem after which they gave three cheers. Private Fairs of the same unit commented in a letter about the Germans singing carols and their bands playing.

It was an extraordinary night for all concerned. The sights and sounds were treasured and particularly memorable for the British were the Christmas trees- Lieutenant Cave (RWR) told his family that "they had their Christmas trees blazing all night." German star shells lit up the sky which for Private Charlie Pratt (RWR) from Evesham "lit up the place lovely and then for the first time we saw friend and foe." It had been a "topping night" enthused Major Arthur Bates of the London Rifle Brigade who thought it would, however, be "interesting to see what happens tomorrow".

It would appear that at most truces along the Western Front, it was the German other ranks who made the initial advances. According to Frederic Coleman who was visiting the Somerset Light Infantry trenches "all the first moves come from them, not us. They even said they would fire high if they got orders to fire on us. We didn't make no such foolish promise…"

For the majority in the 11th Brigade's front line, Christmas Eve was a magical moment but not for all- the 11th Brigade War Diary confirms the report that one man of the London Rifle Brigade (Rifleman Bassingham) was killed and two went down sick and also records that one man was wounded in each of the East Lancashires and Somerset Light Infantry and 5 were reported sick in the Hampshires.

CHRISTMAS DAY

Christmas Day : How it dawned for many

Bruce Bairnsfather's depiction of dawn on Christmas Day
©2 014 Estate of Barbara Bruce Littlejohn

At dawn when standing-to-arms, Private Harry Morgan (RWR) noticed one thing in particular: "There was no rapid fire, in fact no firing at all, only an unreal silence. We were all aware of it and those not on duty came out from their dugouts to see why it was so quiet. No guns! No bullets! No voices: Nothing. The spell was broken by the now customary cockcrow from the German trench."

At dawn, Kurt Zehmisch and his 'A' Section wished the Royal Warwicks 'C' Company "Good morning" which was reciprocated: "We stood behind or on the parapets with half or all our body out of the trench. No shots were fired." He met two or three English officers and was able to converse easily with them as he was a languages graduate.

Royal Warwicks in a dugout at St. Yves The Royal
Regiment of Fusiliers Museum (Royal Warwickshire)

It was quite a day for Captain Hamilton's 'A' Company: "I went out and found a Saxon officer of the 134th Saxon Corps who was unarmed, 'Alright now'. We shook hands, and said what we could in double Dutch, arranged a local armistice for 48 hours, and returned to our trenches. This was the signal for the respective soldiers to come out. As far as I can make out this effort of ours extended itself on either side for some considerable distance… Wasey and I went to a concert in 'D' Company's trench, and at about midnight, we attended another in our own. The Black Hat gang (four of his young subalterns) had rigged up an enormous dug out, and had plastered the walls with Tatler pictures of all the latest girls. They had a stove with a teapot singing away, and altogether it was a most enjoyable evening. A very merry

Xmas and a most extraordinary one, but I doubled the sentries after midnight…" It was right that the Captain of a Company should be wary and suspicious…

Just before dawn, word was passed down to Private Roe (ELR) that the Hampshires were fraternising with the Germans: "Impossible, whose leg are you pulling?" he asked. He went down to see for himself, saw the interaction and decided that "there is a Christ after all."

Private Colin Munro (SH) wrote to his wife in Ayr: "We had a great time of it on Christmas Day. We were in the trenches. The Germans came out and we went over halfway and shook hands with them." Another Seaforth Highlander, Jim Davie, told his wife that "on Xmas Day the most funny thing happened, we noticed a white flag going up and then one German getting up on the trench and advanced towards us and of course we began to do likewise as did more of the Germans and we began to exchange Xmas greetings and all sorts, they were giving us fags and drinks… they are saying the Germans were in Warsaw and that the Russians were finished and of course we listened to all and said nothing and before we parted for our trenches again we had agreed that we would not shoot at each other that day and we kept our word there wasn't a shot fired that day." The two accounts do not, however, accord with the Battalion's War Diary: "Several came up towards our trenches in the mist but were ordered back and warned that they would be fired at."

Indeed there was a shortage of Christmas spirit emanating from the Seaforth Highlanders' trenches. Their Commander heard that four of his men had met some Germans, reacted furiously and ordered his Major to send the Germans back to their trenches. He ordered his men not to fire unless they left their trenches. When Serjeant Philpotts (RWR) recalled seeing a German standing on the parapet shouting and waving his arms, and being promptly shot down, the order had been carried out on Boxing Day. Thereafter there was an uneasy calm in that section of the trenches.

When the Royal Irish Fusiliers relieved the Seaforths, they heard about the truce and that the Germans' last words to the Seaforths were: "Tell that mad Irish lot to keep quiet, they are always firing"!

Where to Live—[ADVT.]

IN ONE OF THE CHOICEST LOCALITIES OF NORTHERN FRANCE.

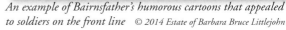

TO BE LET (three minutes from German trenches), this attractive and WELL-BUILT DUG-OUT, containing one reception-kitchen-bedroom and UP-TO-DATE FUNK HOLE (4ft. by 3ft.), all modern inconveniences, including gas and water. This desirable Residence stands one foot above water level, commanding an excellent view of the enemy trenches. EXCELLENT SHOOTING (SNIPE AND DUCK). —Particulars of the late Tenant, Room 6, Base Hospital, Boulog e.

An example of Bairnsfather's humorous cartoons that appealed to soldiers on the front line © 2014 Estate of Barbara Bruce Littlejohn

Despite everything, suspicion and a lack of trust remained. Lieutenant Black (RWR) was referring to his superior, Captain Hamilton: "While I was talking to the officers, crowds of Germans came out and more of my men until we formed a group of about 100 all shaking hands and trying to make each other understood... The Germans outnumbered us by about 4 or 5 to 1 so I told the Captain I thought we had better get back to our trenches which we did after a great deal of bowing." Since the 1/ Royal Warwicks had arrived at Plugstreet Wood on 21st November, they and their Saxon counterparts had been showing each other little mercy- each side had lost many men. And now on Christmas Day, the irony was that they were deferentially bowing to each other!

Private Fairs of the London Rifle Brigade had some interesting news for his parents: "I have had a very funny Christmas. We had an armistice with the Germans and even exchanged cigarettes with them. One gave me a cigar. Funny talking to our foes and walking about in front of the trenches." Another rifleman from the same Brigade considered the Germans to be "very nice chaps... they said they were awfully sick of the war."

The London Rifle Brigade received a visit in the morning from the Bishop of London, Dr. A.F. Winnington-Ingram, their Honorary Chaplain, who was a fervent supporter of the War which he considered a "great crusade to defend the weak against the strong". His anti-German tone in his writings and sermons was criticised by the Prime Minister Herbert Asquith for being "jingoism of the shallowest kind."

Over the Christmas period British soldiers at the Front were delivered a Christmas present from King George V's daughter Princess Mary. David Lloyd-Burch of the 10th Field Ambulance deployed in the Plugstreet area was impressed that at a parade on Christmas morning, their Commanding Officer Colonel Prophet handed out "Princess Mary's gift with Christmas cards". It was an embossed box, which according to Private Harry Morgan (RWR) contained "a pipe, six cigarettes, an ounce of tobacco, a tinder lighter, a Christmas card and a photograph of the Princess and the King." The author Henry Williamson wrote to his mother: "In my mouth is a pipe presented by Princess Mary... In the pipe is German tobacco. Ha Ha, you say, from a prisoner or found in a captured trench. O, dear, no! From a German soldier. Yes a live German soldier from his own trench." For those in the trenches it was a welcome morale-booster and large numbers of the gifts were proudly sent home as keep-sakes."

It was the lack of thunderous artillery fire and the ensuing calm that left a huge impression on, for example, William Tapp (RWR). His day started at 7.40 a.m. when his first duty as an officer's batman was to serve Lieutenant Tillyer with his breakfast: "You know Sir, I miss the sounds of shots flying over, it's like a clock that has stopped ticking."

For those not in the front line trenches, Christmas celebrations were relaxed and not tinged with any suspicious feelings. In the evening Private Edward Packe (SLI) went into a cottage near Somerset Farm where "there is a family living (only a mile from the firing line) and had a sort of sing-song, the French (he should have written Belgian!) sung one and then we'd sing one. It was rather a mixture, carols and 'Tipperary' being mixed together." On the whole Packe had "a jolly good Christmas" and he hoped "you all enjoyed yours as much."

A couple of Saxons in front of the Rifle Brigade were, according to Frederic Coleman, unhappy with the spirit of friendliness pervading No Man's Land, one "wouldn't have no truce… He kept hammerin' away all through the piece no matter what the Saxon chaps in front of us did." He also related that some Somersets

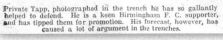

Private Tapp, photographed in the trench he has so gallantly helped to defend. He is a keen Birmingham F. C. supporter, and has tipped them for promotion. His forecast, however, has caused a lot of argument in the trenches.

Private William Tapp, Lieutenant Tillyer's batman, cooking breakfast
The Birmingham Post's Picture World 10th March 1915

who approached a Saxon trench were confronted by "a stocky little heavy-set German officer with a bushy black beard who said with a scowl like he was goin' to eat us: 'Get back to your trenches, we have had quite enough of you. Get back there at once.'"

At the time when Tommy and Fritz were meeting in No Man's Land, Generals French, Haig and Smith-Dorrien were lunching in St. Omer: "We were ordered to form Armies tomorrow" wrote Haig. "I am to command the First, Smith-Dorrien the Second."

To what extent was High Command aware of what had happened on Christmas Day? A message was sent from Brigadier General Hunter-Weston of the 11th Brigade to Brigadier General Hull of the 10th Brigade: "Would it not be a good thing if the two officers commanding the Battalions of your right section and the officer commanding the Somersets were to meet you and I at your Head Quarters or ours whichever is most convenient to you at any time tomorrow?" This was sent at 3.55 in the afternoon, as the light faded after an extraordinary day. He appears to be referring to Major A.J. Poole of the Royal Warwicks, Lieutenant Colonel Arthur Loveband o the Royal Dublin Fusilliers and Major Compton of the Somerset Light Infantry. Were the Generals in the process of hauling in commanders in the trenches to explain themselves? Unfortunately there is little evidence of the suggested meeting having taken place or any disciplinary action invoked.

EXCHANGES

The most common and popularly received items swapped in No Man's Land were German cigars and English cigarettes. Literally millions of cigarettes were smoked by British soldiers on the Western Front. Captain Hamilton (RWR) often received parcels from his wife Irene containing tobacco and 200 cigarettes. Smoking helped soldiers to relax in the trenches and formed a bond between them. It was natural that cigarettes should feature prominently in No Man's Land exchanges and that smoking should have been central to Tommy and Fritz's festive socialisation.

Captain Hamilton and his subalterns delighted in a quiet, reflective time smoking German cigars in his dugout on Boxing Day evening!

Some examples of items swapped:

RSM George Beck (RWR):	"Germans were very eager to exchange almost anything for our bully beef and jam"
Lieut. Cave (RWR):	He received a piece of iron cross ribbon, a photo of Germans in a group and a programme of carols issued to every man on Christmas Eve
Pte. Alfred Day (RWR):	He and Germans signed and addressed postcards
Pte. B. Hutchings (HR):	The German drew a cap badge which was given to him with a cigar "in exchange for my own…"
Pte. Harry Morgan (RWR):	Negotiated a cigarette case for a tin of bully beef
Pte Colin Munro (SH):	"We exchanged knives, pipes and postcards. I got a knife, three cigars and a postcard. I got some of the Germans to sign their names and the postcard I now send to you (his wife) as a keepsake."
Pte. W. Pentelow (RB):	"I had seven cigars and several cigarettes from them. I also gave a few of them my home address."
Pte. Edward Roe (ELR):	"They gave us bottles of wine and cigars, we gave them tins of jam, bully, mufflers, tobacco etc. I annexed a tin of raspberry from the sergeant's dugout and gave it to a stodgy and bespectacled Saxon. In return he gave me a leather case containing five cigars."

Pte. William Tapp (RWR):   He received two buttons, a cap badge, five rounds of ammunition and coins- "I pull a button off my coat and he does the same"

There was regret over one exchange. The Wray brothers of the London Rifle Brigade heard a voice calling out from the German trenches on Boxing Day: "I want to speak to an officer… yesterday I gave my hat for bully beef… I have a grand inspection tomorrow… you lend me and I bring it back to you." The loan was made and the pact kept, sealed with a tin of bully!

Frederic Coleman wrote that an exchange of rations was a frequent occurrence and both sides agreed that tinned "bully" had no serious rival. Tinned meat had to be served as nothing could be cooked near the trenches for fear of smoke giving the enemy a target and Edward Packe (SLI) informed his family in a letter that over Christmas "a fire in the trench was only possible because of the truce."

Some missed out. Private A. Barnett (RWR) wrote that "some of our men got hold of some souvenirs, but I failed to manage one myself."

The majority of those who participated in the No Man's Land "bring and swap" sessions, were no doubt blissfully unaware of "Instructions to be issued to formations and individuals

A MEMORY OF CHRISTMAS, 1914: "LOOK AT THIS BLOKE'S BUTTONS, 'ARRY. I SHOULD RECKON 'E 'AS A MAID TO DRESS 'IM"

Christmas Day Exchanges by Bruce Bairnsfather. The artist is in the middle- he used his barbed-wire cutters to swap buttons with a German officer   © 2014 Estate of Barbara Bruce Littlejohn

landing in this country" which were published at the outset of the campaign in August: "Men must be warned not to give away or sell any of the badges, clasps, knives etc. because it is contrary to discipline and they will be punished." At least an army issue knife was not one of William Tapp's items for barter- when out for a stroll he met a few Germans who wanted to buy an army knife from him: "I don't want to sell mine" was his response.

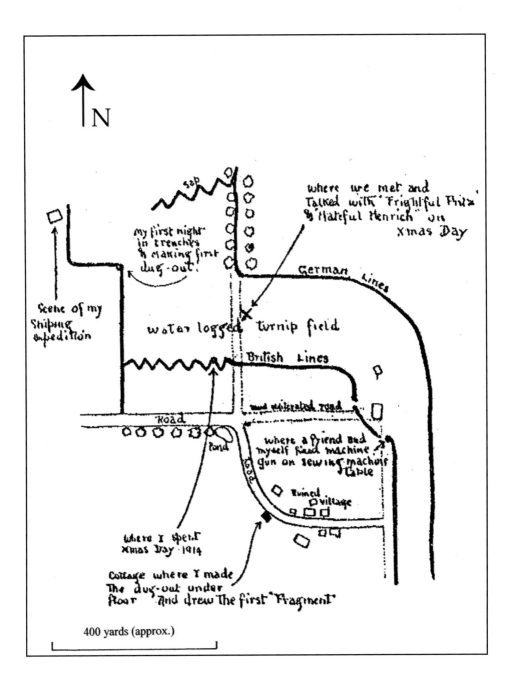

N

where we met and
Talked with "Frightful Fritz"
& "Hateful Henrich" on
Xmas Day

sap

my first night
in trenches
& making first
dug-out!

German Lines

Scene of my
Sniping
expedition

water logged turnip field

British Lines

mud obliterated road

Road

Pond

where a friend and
myself fixed machine
gun on sewing machine
table

Ruined
village

where I spent
Xmas Day 1914

Cottage where I made
The dug-out under
floor And drew The first "Fragment"

400 yards (approx.)

**MAP V
LOCATION OF
LIEUTENANT BRUCE BAIRNSFATHER'S CHRISTMAS TRUCE**

COMMUNICATION

Several British soldiers were impressed by the Germans' command of the English language, particularly when shouting out festive messages from the trenches. It was far superior to their limited, if non-existent German. Not much has changed! Private Layton (RWR) was impressed that "a good many of them could speak broken English all right." Tapp noticed that "quite a lot can talk English" and a colleague considered it noteworthy that "some of the Germans spoke English very well, so they shouted 'no shoot' and we said the same." Private Harry Morgan (RWR) remembered a German soldier shouting out "Come over here Warwicks" in "absolutely perfect English." Corporal Cook (SLI)) had a chat with several Germans and remarked that "quite a lot of them can speak fair English."

Rifleman Reading (RB) in a letter to his wife confessed to being impressed with how on Christmas Day the Germans sang and shouted "all in good English" especially: "Are you the Rifle Brigade, have you a spare bottle? If so, we will come half way and you come the other half."

The Somersets found the Saxons were "friendly enough": in one conversation, a German said "You are Anglo-Saxons, we Saxons. We not want to fight you." A bandsman claimed to have asked "What about the Kaiser then old lad? What do you think of the Kaiser, eh?" 'Bring him here and we'll shoot him for you' said the Saxon feller and we all laughed." Corporal John Ferguson (SH)) spoke to "Fritz in a group of Germans" who occasionally translated to his friends what he was saying.

In contrast, some of the British officers who engaged in face to face discussions with their adversaries had to resort to other modes of communication. Lieutenant Drummond of the Royal Field Artillery talked to Germans mainly in French "because my German was not very good, and none of the Germans could speak English well." Captain Hamilton and his counterpart when in No Man's Land said what they could in "double Dutch". Languages graduate Kurt Zehmisch, however, was able to conduct "a delightful conversation in English, French or German" with several English officers.

GERMANS

The 11th Brigade War Diary reported: "From conversations today between our men and the Germans in front of us, it is quite clear that they are still part of the XIX Corps- they are Saxons from Chemnitz" and that "the enemy belonged to the 132nd, 133rd, and 134th Regts of XIXth Saxon Corps." A detailed note from 4th Division to III Corps mentions that information was gained on 25th December "that in front of the Division there were 133rd Regiment from Le Gheer to below St. Yves and 134th Regiment from below St. Yves to La Douve Farm."

Unlike most of the British Expeditionary Force at this early stage of the War, the German Army consisted mainly of conscripts; many were reluctant soldiers, weary of conditions in the trenches and the dangers they faced. They were part of an unwelcome invading army, despised by the local population- all of which heightened their desire to engage in a ceasefire and a peaceful celebration of Christmas.

A German soldier in a trench looking at what may be an unexploded British shell   South West Heritage Trust

A number of those who were able to communicate with the Germans they met, refer to their morale and state of mind. Lieutenant Black (RWR) considered the Germans "are just as tired of the War as we are…" Private Alfred Day (RWR) wrote in the same vein that "they will be glad when the War is over" and Private Layton (RWR) claimed that "one or two wanted to be taken prisoner."

William Tapp (RWR) was of the opinion that the Germans seemed "a decent lot of fellows"- the British were generally better disposed towards the Saxons than Prussians whom Captain Hamilton described as "treacherous". It is questionable as to whether there would have been the same level of "high jinks" if the Prussians had been entrenched opposite them.

Captain Hamilton felt from his conversations that the German officers were upbeat about their situation; he was told by them that the Russians were washed out, the British had their own problems with the Irish and "the French they laugh at." Private Pentelow (RB) got the impression that the Germans were "fed up and will be glad when it is over." His account, like a number of others, commented that some of the Germans were old and others "quite boys".

Lieutenant Cyril Drummond (RFA) met a group of Germans and described them as "very nice fellows to look at, they looked more like university students than soldiers, and one of them said 'We don't want to kill you, and you don't want to kill us. So why shoot?'"

The Germans met by the London Rifle Brigade were "a fine set of fellows" recorded Lance Corporal Calder and "many could talk good English." Henry Williamson described the Saxons he met as "Landsturmers or Landwehr and Saxons and Bavarians… Many are gentle looking men… and some are very big and arrogant looking… many of the Germans here are, or were, waiters (in England)." He was also keen to point out that there were no popular Prussians.

Another London Rifle Brigade account by Rifleman Percy states that "they were really magnificent in the whole thing, and jolly good sorts. I have now a very different opinion of the Germans."

According to Captain J.D.M. Beckett of the 1/ Hampshires, the Germans "seemed very simple-minded creatures, and were much elated over alleged victories in Russia. They stated they wished the war would soon finish, but were confident of their success."

Bruce Bairnsfather would have been amused to learn that there was a German cartoonist in action, drawing sketches behing their lines! the cartoon on the wall shows, from the right, German soldiers cheering, Germans shooting and the French soldiers in retreat. The caption reads "The Fright of the French"
In Flanders Fields Museum, Ypres

FOOTBALL

The Christmas Truce has become synonymous with games of football. Media coverage in a World Cup year, 2014, has emphasised the game's ability to bring nations together and that the match at St. Yves was one of the few bright moments of peace and humanity during the most horrendous of wars. This year football matches at Messines and St. Yves will commemorate the events of 1914. It is understandable that local authorities in Flemish Messines and French-speaking Comines-Warneton should wish to lay claim to 'international' football matches played in 1914 to promote tourism in their district as well as marking the centenary. When they kick off, will they be commemorating an England v Germany game that really took place in the area in 1914, supported by hard evidence?

RSM George Beck (RWR) asserted that "the Germans ask to play football." Private William Tapp supported Birmingham City and was a keen player. He would have been excited by the prospect of a match against his enemies and his diary entry for Christmas Day records that "we are trying to arrange a football match for Boxing Day." He was fearful that the Royal Field Artillery, which took little or no notice of what happened in front of them, could scupper the match. A mere Private, he would not have been privy to officers' discussions about a match, which were positive but ultimately unsuccessful.

Leutnant Zehmisch's recollection was that "a couple of English brought a football out of a trench and a vigorous football match began," one assumes amongst themselves or does he mean that some Saxons joined in? He continued: "This was all so marvellous and strange. The English officers thought so too. Towards evening the officers asked whether a big football match could be held on the following day between the two positions. However, we were unable to agree definitely to this, because, as we told them, a new captain would be there the next day. Towards evening we parted with hearty handshakes and returned to our trenches." At 7 o'clock in the evening Zehmisch and his unit were relieved.

So William Tapp would have been disappointed but Zehmisch's reason is corroborated by Hamilton: "'A' Company would have played the 134th Saxon Corps tomorrow, only that the company was relieved." An extract from a letter home from Private Walter Cooke explains to his parents that the Germans "wanted to play at football but that fell through." Lance Corporal Coulson (LRB) was probably referring to the aborted Royal Warwicks' match when he wrote that "one regiment I hear, tried to arrange a football match for this afternoon, but I don't think that came off," a fact confirmed by Major Hawksley (RFA) who was with the Royal Warwicks over Christmas, although he maintained that "our authorities stopped it."

So what, if anything, did take place? Bruce Bairnsfather provides the answer. In his *Bullets and Bullets* he states that at "about noon as the general laxity and friendliness were growing, a football match was suggested. Someone had evidently received a deflated football as a Christmas present" and in an interview given to a Canadian TV company in 1958 he

Captain Robert Hamilton's diary entry for Christmas Day in which he makes it clear that a proposed football match could not take place   Andrew Hamilton

recalled that the football was inflated and a kick around ensued amongst the 1/ Royal Warwicks. He does not suggest that any Germans joined in.

In a letter written on Boxing Day, Private Smith (RWR)) tells of how he and others on Christmas Day afternoon "even played football between the two lines of trenches" (i.e. in No Man's Land). The Germans he added "were interested spectators." Private William Setchfield was a keen goalkeeper and Nottingham Forest supporter- however he does not mention in his letters home any actual match played against the Germans. One can conclude, therefore, that the evidence hardly confirms that there was an Anglo/ German football match at St. Yves involving the Royal Warwicks. At best, some of the Germans might have kicked a miss-placed pass back to their foes! It is a case, we believe, of the adage "never let the truth get in the way of a good story"!

Major General Sir Frederick Maurice in his *History of the London Rifle Brigade* written in 1921, maintained that there had been "rumours of a proposed football match but the authorities frowned upon ideas of this sort and stopped them, quite rightly because it would have been most unwise to allow the Germans to know how weakly the British trenches were held." Serjeant Hugh Wilson (RIF) heard that the Germans wanted to arrange a football match but the Seaforths' Commanding Officer refused to sanction it.

Despite Major General Maurice's view, there is a reference to a game of football taking place in the Plugstreet Wood area, involving the London Rifle Brigade. Its reliability is open to question. W.R.M. Percy (LRB) mentions that on Christmas Day a football match was played "between them and us in front of the trench." If a game did take place, it is strange that none of the many accounts of Christmas time at Plugstreet Wood refer to an event, news of which must surely have spread like wildfire round the other battalions in the vicinity.

The authors at the Khaki Chums' Cross near Prowse Point. Footballs have overrun the Cross which was intended by the Khaki Chums (The Association of Military Remembrance) to commemorate the Christmas Truce in general, not a non-existent international football match at St. Yves!   Annette George

It is possible that a game may have taken place involving the 133rd Saxon Regiment. One of their soldiers called Albert, wrote home on 15th January: "Happy to have received parcel no. 2. I wish you a belated Merry Christmas; I was allowed to celebrate in the trenches where we set up a little Christmas tree. There was a ceasefire during which we exchanged tobacco and played ball with Tommy." This game may have taken place a few kilometres from Plugstreet Wood in the Frelinghien area. Leutnant Johannes Niemann recorded that a soldier in a Scottish Battalion produced a football and "now there developed a proper game of football with caps put down as goalposts. Quite a happening on that frozen field. One of us had a camera on him. So both teams quickly organised themselves into one group, a fine motley crew with the football in the middle. The game ended 3-2 to Fritz.

During this football game our lancers had soon discovered that the Scots wore no underpants beneath their kilts, so that their backsides were clearly visible as soon as their kilts started flapping. This delighted us hugely, and we were both loathe to believe it at first, until we were informed by the other side themselves. I learnt this for myself again later in a practical way when I was lying seriously wounded on the floor of an English ambulance and sitting above me on a perch were four lightly wounded Scots. There I could again confirm that they wore nothing underneath!"

A letter in *The Times* by a Major in the RAMC starts "this has been a strange Christmas" and he claims that "the _____ Regiment actually had a football match with the Saxons who beat them 3-2!!!"

The Commanding Officer of the 1/ East Lancashires, Lieutenant Colonel G. H. Lawrence told the Germans he encountered that "if they would have an armistice on New Year's Day we would play them at football between our lines- so that remains to be seen… should it come off, it will be a funny sight as I will keep half my men armed and ready in the trenches, while the others would be encouraging their side. I wonder if it will come off…" but unfortunately "we never got our football match, the Germans were not for it and sniped all day." This is corroborated in the memoir of Lieutenant (later Brigadier) C.E.M. Richards (ELR) who recalled that "I received a signal from Battalion Headquarters telling me to make a football pitch in No Man's Land by filling up shell-holes etc. and to challenge the enemy to a Football Match on 1st January. I was furious and took no notice at all… The proposed match did not take place."

However, an extraordinary thing happened- Major General H.F.M. Wilson of the 4th Division and his staff according to Lawrence "turned up at 11.00 a.m. to see it (the match) but were disappointed, as were various other fellows who turned up. As they would not play, we shelled their trenches!"

Elsewhere on the Western Front, few 'internationals' took place substantiated by compelling evidence. A Peter Jackson initiated a match in his section: "After a short while somebody punted across a football. The ball landed amongst the Germans and they immediately kicked it back at our men. And after a while of milling around with a football it seemed to me that there would be another free fight beginning so I suggested that we had a football match. And it was a mêlée. It wasn't a question of ten aside, it was a question of 70 Germans against 50 Englishmen. And they were kicking the ball backwards and forwards to the trenches, to the barbed wire for quite half an hour until unfortunately the ball got impaled on one of the stakes of the barbed wire and was deflated. And that put an end to the football match."

There was without question a spontaneous kick-about at St. Yves amongst the Royal Warwicks with Saxons looking on as interested spectators, some of whom may have joined in a small kick about rather than the suggested 'big' football match Zehmisch mentioned. There may have been a match involving the London Rifle Brigade but we have only seen one short account and no references to it by soldiers from the other battalions at Plugstreet Wood. The point also has to made that conditions in No Man's Land were hardly conducive for a proper match- mud and flooded shell craters meant that flat areas were at a premium.

CHRISTMAS FAYRE

What would Christmas Day be without a hearty lunch of turkey and all the trimmings? The troops in the trenches were determined not to miss out. Richard Lintott (LRB) was concerned that a Christmas pudding he had requested, should be sent as soon as possible "or else it might not reach me in time for Christmas." He was unsure as to whether he would be in the trenches but in a later letter reported he was "in some breastworks in the woods in support." His Christmas dinner there consisted of "stewed rabbit, rashers" and one assumes his pudding, all of which he admitted "was not so bad in the circumstances." Private Walter Cooke (RWR) sent thanks for "the plum duff and mince pies" which were "a treat". He and his chums "had a real good feed on Christmas Day; we had a duck for our Christmas dinner. We bought it off a Belgian farmer for 5 francs. We plucked it and cleaned it ourselves, and roasted it in bacon fat." Private Alfred Smith's letter home must have caused a stir when he wrote a letter to his wife on a paper serviette: "I daresay you will be surprised at me writing a letter on such paper as this, but you will be more surprised when I tell you that it contained cake given to one of our men by a German officer on Christmas Day and I was given some of it." William Tapp congratulated himself on the superb Christmas lunch he and fellow officers' servants had concocted. He expressed the hope that "everyone back home has as good food for their Christmas Day." Rifleman Ernest Furneaux (RB) "had a nice dinner- I made it myself- stew, potatoes, carrots, turnips and meat which we had out of a garden nearby and of course pudding."

Private Edward Packe (SLI) "tackled the Plum Pudding on the spot, ten people had a bit but it was mostly shared by four of us and after giving some away there was about a quarter left which contained the three penny piece. So cutting it into four we each had a piece. I had the last which did contain one three pence so I maintained my reputation for always getting the three pence."

Private Fairs (LRB) was delighted with his Boxing Day food: "Our menu for breakfast was sardines, biscuits, butter and jam and for dinner, tinned meat and Christmas pudding."

A slap-up Christmas dinner could only raise spirits on a cold and frosty morning in the trenches- a reward for months of danger and discomfort and a meal to be enjoyed in peace and quiet, free from shells and snipers… the only thing missing for all those feasting in the trenches was the traditional turkey and trimmings!

Strange Happenings and Coincidences

One of the most remarkable coincidences to occur in the trenches at St. Yves involved Captain Robert Hamilton. He had fought during the Boer War with the Norfolk Regiment before his transfer to the Royal Warwicks. In 1912 he attended a Norfolks' regimental dinner at the Trocadero restaurant in London's Mayfair; he clearly enjoyed the evening, ticking off on the menu the wines and liqueurs he imbibed, the many courses he sampled and he noted when he took time out to smoke cigars and cigarettes. Two years later in No Man's Land "the chef of the Trocadero was among the Saxons in front of us, and he seemed delighted to meet some of his former clients"!

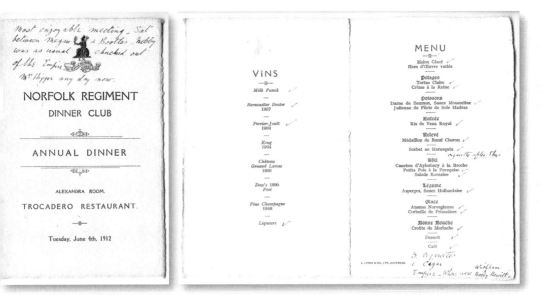

The menu card for Captain Robert Hamilton's Norfolk Regimental Dinner at the Trocadero Restaurant, in Piccadilly, London. He met the German chef in No Man's Land on Christmas Day 1914!
Andrew Hamilton

Several of the Royal Warwicks met a German who had worked as a waiter in Eastbourne for ten years who wished he was back there. Many Germans were based in England before the War. Private Day (RWR) met several who had lived in London. According to Rifleman Jack Chappell (LRB), his friend Russell "was introduced to a barber in the Strand named Liddle." Serjeant Philpotts (RWR) spoke to a German chef from Birmingham who at the outbreak of war had been forced to leave his wife and five children when called up for front line action. Philpotts recounted for the 1964 BBC Great War Series how, when hostilities resumed in January 1915, a voice could be heard loud and clear from the German line: "'Are you the Warwicks? Any Brummagem lads there? I have a wife and five kids in Brummagem.' Our company wag who in civil life was a policeman, called

Coiffure in the Trenches.
"Keep yer 'ead still, or I'll 'ave yer blinkin' ear off."

Coiffure in the trenches by Bruce Bairnsfather
© 2014 Estate of Barbara Bruce Littlejohn

back: 'yes mate and if you don't get your head down, there'll be a widow and five orphans in Brummagem'!"

Private B. Hutchings (HR) recalled that when in No Man's Land he met "a nice fellow… We shook hands and his first words to me was were there any Scotch territorials out yet as he himself was a waiter in Glasgow."

Harry Morgan, Private Mattey and Lieutenant Bruce Bairnsfather, all of the Royal Warwicks, enjoyed the bizarre spectacle of Jack Reagan, a machine-gunner, cutting the lengthy locks of a Saxon who was patiently kneeling on the ground! Bairnsfather captured a similar moment in one of his inimitable cartoons which depicts a Tommy having his hair cut.

Cratered ground around St. Yves not ideal for an international England v Germany football match!
The Royal Regiment of Fusiliers Museum (Royal Warwickshire)

H.G.R. Williams (LRB) a German speaker recounted a bizarre experience on New Year's Eve: "I found a large and drunk German actually in our trench, brandishing a bottle of beer in each hand, and pressing all and sundry to have a drink. Our officer was perturbed at the idea of having this enemy actually IN our trench and wished me to explain to him that he really should have been made a prisoner, but that we did not want to spoil the atmosphere of the truce, by doing this and that *he really must go home!*

I tried to explain this but he was far too drunk to take it in. I asked him if he did want to become a prisoner to which he replied: 'Ach Gott, nein', nor could I persuade him to leave voluntarily. The

German caught in wire in No Man's Land by Bruce Bairnsfather © *2014 Estate of Barbara Bruce Littlejohn*

whole situation struck me as fantastic. Here we are in the middle of a war, beseeching one of the enemy to leave our trench and go back to his own!

In the end he had to be escorted back by two men, of whom I was one, we proceeded across No Man's Land, one taking each of his arms, while he sang happily and bawdily, and left him at the gap in the German wire…"

One of the most bizarre questions to be asked in No Man's Land get-togethers was related by Captain J.R. Somers-Smith of the London Rifle Brigade and asked of him in all seriousness by one of several Germans who genuinely believed that London had been taken: "By how many Germans was London taken?"

A motivating factor for many volunteers to enlist at the outset of the War, had been the shocking treatment by the Germans of civilians in Belgian towns like Aerschot, Dinant and Louvain between 19th and 25th August 1914. In the second typed up version of his diary, Arthur Cook (SLI) told of how, when behind the lines over Christmas, he walked round Ploegsteert and noticed the "fruits" of how "the Germans made sinister use of their time here, for all the young maidens from eleven upwards appear to have been raped and are showing signs of motherhood."

A strange happening for many in the trenches was the arrival of "Top Brass" over the Christmas period. Private Roe (ELR) waspishly encapsulated the feelings of the typical Tommy in the trenches: "Members of the Regimental staff, who in times of turmoil and strife gave the trenches a wide berth, now that the truce was on, got quite bold and came up to inspect our trenches, just to see how we lived- and died." **61**

GROUP PHOTOGRAPHS

Every major event nowadays will be instantly recorded by a host of mobile phones- the Last Post Ceremony at the Menin Gate is a sea of outstretched arms recording it. In No Man's Land at Plugstreet Wood, participants also wanted to capture the

moment for posterity. There are several instances of mixed groups of English and Germans being snapped by small box cameras. NCO Holland, under the command of Leutnant Zehmisch took "three photographs of us in groups with the English."

On Christmas Day Rifleman Turner of the London Rifle Brigade took a number of photographs with a pocket camera, of Saxons and his comrades in No Man's Land.

Photograph taken by Leutnant Zehmisch of NCO Holland with the booty he captured from a British trench- coat, rifle, bayonet and a cap possibly with the Royal Warwicks' antelope cap badge In Flanders Fields Museum, Ypres

Private William Setchfield (RWR) informed his family that "the Germans came over to us in the afternoon and we had our photos taken with them…"

Lieutenant Cave (RWR) was one of a group photograph of "Germans and Tommies together and officers. The Germans have promised to bring me a print of it tomorrow at midnight." It would appear that it was delivered as promised- in a letter dated 31st December, he mentions that he has "enclosed a piece of iron cross ribbon given to him by a corporal of the 6th Jäger Regiment as well as a photo of Germans given to him by the officer who is in the centre of the picture." This begs the question as to how and when the photographs were developed in such a short time...

Rifleman Percy (LRB) writes that "one of the German officers took a photo of English and German soldiers arm-in-arm with exchanged caps and helmets."

Sadly only photographs of two meetings taken at Plugstreet

Riflemen Andrew and Grigg (LRB) standing behind the German, who is wearing a pickelhaube. The photograph is one of several taken by Rifleman Turner IWM Q70075

Wood are known to have survived, one of which was taken by Lieutenant Cyril Drummond of the Royal Field Artillery. On hearing of strange happenings in No Man's Land, he brought his camera with him on Boxing Day and photographed a group of 1/ Royal Warwicks (including an officer) and soldiers of the 134th Saxon Regiment: "I lined them all up and took a photograph."

Lieutenant Cyril Drummond's photograph of the Royal Warwicks and 134th Saxon Regiment on Boxing Day in No Man's Land by the sunken road at St. Yves Second left is a British officer and fourth and fifth from left are Tommies. (Map VI = 3F-2)   IWM HU35801

The site of Drummond's photo- the line of German trenches would have been halfway towards Bayern Farmhouse   Andrew Hamilton

INTELLIGENCE GATHERING

Brigade and Battalion War Diaries justified the Truce by emphasising how much information had been gathered during the fraternisations. To what extent the reports soothed the ire of General Smith-Dorrien, the newly installed Commander in Chief of the Second Army, is difficult to gauge. The 10th Brigade War Diary reported that "some valuable information was gleaned during the intercourse. The trenches seem fairly strongly held, the enemy cheerful and well fed."

The Commanding Officer of the 1/ East Lancashires, Lieutenant Colonel G. H. Lawrence, provides us with an extraordinary account. He must have been one of very few COs to visit the German trenches over the period of the truce. He justified the meetings in No Man's Land as an opportunity to find out information about the enemy: "At 10.00 a.m. on Christmas Day I went round all the trenches and wished men a Happy Xmas… there was a sudden hurrah and rush and our men and the Germans started running to one another and meeting half way, shook hands. I did not like it at first and ordered my men back, then was told the Germans wanted a truce to bury their dead, so I agreed. Ordering half the men to keep a smart look out in the trenches with their rifles ready, I went forward and joined the crowd… for an hour I stood there and took the opportunity of observing their trenches and sent my Subs to other parts of the line to observe while I kept their men away from our trenches and we got useful information." He observed German trenches but refused to allow the Germans near his… his superiors in the Brigade and Division would have been impressed but was he being economical with the truth?

Information garnered for the Royal Warwicks' War Diary included details of the Germans' cooking arrangements, that "they stay in advance trenches for only one night, barbed wire is of only one kind, snipers wear distinctive uniform and they carry a lamp on their chest."

According to Frederic Coleman he and others "wanted to see the German trenches bad. They wouldn't let us right in, but we saw and learned a lot. We could get right up to their wire, which was no end better than ours. But it ain't now. Wait till they try goin' against our wire, and they will find we learned a thing or two."

Captain Beckett (HR) reported to 11th Brigade Head Quarters about the events of Christmas Day. He noted a number of things he had observed. The men were between the ages of 19 and 45, were well clothed and seemed well supplied and every soldier was wearing gum boots. The Germans' trenches were in good condition and relatively free from water. Loopholes (through which rifles were fired) were 18 inches from ground level and about ten feet apart. How he came across such information is hard to judge given that he had kept his men from contact with the enemy.

The 11th Brigade Diary emphatically states that "the Germans were not allowed near our lines" but conversely claims that "several of our officers visited the German trenches, most of which were well made but partly full of water." A lot of the enemy were apparently wearing gum boots: "Much valuable information was gained with regard to the enemy's wire entanglements." Does one detect a certain disingenuousness by the author? Would the officers really have been welcomed into the German trenches and that there was not a reciprocal arrangement? One suspects that German officers had also been visiting British trenches; no self- respecting British officer would have admitted to that. It is interesting that there are few references to information gathering in any of the officers' private accounts.

At Divisional level it was recorded that "we acquired a certain amount of information, the principal item being that to our surprise the enemy are holding their trenches in greater strength than we thought and also than we are. Their trenches appear to be wetter than ours, but their wire entanglements are undoubtedly better than ours."

It does seem unlikely that either side would have allowed their enemies to approach too near their own trenches- much depended on the decision of the Commanding Officer. Private Edward Packe's Somerset Light Infantry CO must have been opposed to any fraternisation as he asserted that the Germans "were not allowed near our trenches and they wouldn't allow us near theirs... the bare fact is I think we each advanced into the middle and hobnobbed there."

"Making Good"

Any work to trenches prior to Christmas had been fraught with danger- a moment's lapse in concentration and a sniper's bullet from the opposing trench, a hundred yards away or less, (Lieutenant Cave in a letter described the gap as being just 70 yards) would be deadly. The officers in the forward trenches saw the armistice as an opportunity to carry out important works and took executive decisions to do so. Lieutenant Cave emphasised the importance of the Christmas break in hostilities: "We take the opportunity of improving our trenches, making good out parapets and putting up our barbed wire entanglements in full view of the enemy." Tapp's officer Lieutenant Tillyer had "taken advantage of the lull, he has kept the men working and made our trench like a fort." In his opinion, the Germans

A fatigue party in Hunter Avenue
South West Heritage Trust

"do not seem to be doing so much at theirs" presumably because their construction was superior- not just in 1914 but for the rest of the War when, for example, they withstood the pre-attack bombardment on 1st July 1916 on the Somme. Boxing Day was spent by many of the Somersets strengthening their trench defences.

The 9th Field Company of the Royal Engineers were granted a break from such duties on Christmas Day. On Boxing Day they were back working on barbed wire improvements in front of the Royal Warwicks' trenches.

There is surprisingly little mention of "making good" in the official War Diaries apart from a mention on New Year's Day in the Somerset Light Infantry War Diary of a brushwood screen being made "in order that when placed in suitable spots, access to the forward trenches becomes possible without being observed by the enemy."

Trench digging   South West Heritage Trust

66

COLLECTION OF BODIES AND BURIALS

Major General Sir Frederick Maurice wrote in the *History of the Rifle Brigade* that the Christmas Truce was essentially a question of proper respect to the dead. Both sides welcomed the chance to bring in their dead from in between the lines and bury them nearby. The 10th Brigade War Diary recorded that "3 men of the Somerset Light Infantry, 3 Germans of the 134th Saxons, 3 Hampshires, one Prussian and an Uhlan were all buried. The Germans helped in the digging, the 1/ Royal Warwicks supplied the tools" as the Germans unconvincingly "stated they had no spades."

Serjeant Philpotts (RWR) saw three Germans approaching with a Red Cross and called out: "As it is a holy Christmas, we will allow you to bury your dead." He continued "just to our right were over 50 dead of the Somerset Light Infantry who had been killed attempting to straighten our line (six days earlier on 19 December). The Germans helped us dig a huge grave on the edge of Plugstreet Wood and a proper military funeral took place."

The 11th Brigade Battalions and the opposing Germans also collected and buried each other's dead. Rifleman Jack Chappell (LRB) recalled that "both sides then buried their dead whom they had not been able to get to before." The greatest losses during the attack on 19th December had been suffered by the 1/ Somerset Light Infantry, twelve of whom had been killed by "friendly fire." The bodies of Captains Maud and Orr and Lieutenant Henson were collected as well as those of 18 NCOs and other ranks. A Saxon officer commented that Captain Maud was "the bravest of the brave". Frederic Coleman quoted a bandsman who considered "our medical officer is a funny cove, and he got an idea in his head that started the whole thing. He said he saw a chance to give a burial to some of our dead… So he told me and my pal to follow him…The Saxons was right there in plain sight. I never did sweat so, nor did my pal here. Some of our dead… was in an awful state… No one fired a single shot…" To the right, "some of our lads were going right over to the Bosches in the open," as a result of which the Somerset Light Infantry's Commanding Officer allowed men to go out who, the Germans agreed, could bury the dead until 4 o'clock. Burials took place in Plugstreet Wood near Somerset House, the Battalion's Headquarters. It is now the Ploegsteert Wood Military Cemetery.

When David Lloyd-Burch of the 10th Field Ambulance heard that troops were holding a truce, he went down to the trenches where he found both sets of troops burying their dead between the trenches. Private Edward Packe (SLI) was in support trenches and was told by stretcher-bearers that "you couldn't hear a shot fired the whole day anywhere and it was awfully hard to realise there was a war on until they came for a fatigue party from our company to bury the dead they had brought in." **67**

In his report to the 11th Brigade, Captain Beckett of the 1/Hampshire wrote that the "enemy asked that they should be allowed to bury their dead of which there were a considerable number a short way from their trench." He granted this request as by this time considerable numbers were walking about their trenches and it would have been difficult to round them up and order them back. A boundary line was agreed beyond which the Germans were not to go.

The East Lancashires were grateful for the chance to fix the problem of dead bodies- according to Private Edward Roe, some Saxons had been lying in No Man's Land in a mangel-wurzel field since "we made our first counter-attack in October." He and his comrades were thankful as when the wind blew in their direction "it made us sick with the foetid atmosphere of decaying bodies."

Rifleman Henry Williamson (LRB), wrote: "All Christmas Day grey and khaki figures mingled and talked in No Man's Land. Picks and spades rang in the hard ground. It was strange to stare at the dead we had only glimpsed, swiftly, from the trenches. The shallowest graves were dug, filled, and set with crosses knocked together from lengths of ration-box wood, marked with indelible pencil. 'For King and Country.' 'Für Vaterland und Freiheit'." (For Fatherland and Freedom)

Lieutenant Cave (RWR) admitted in a letter that he was glad that the dead had been brought in as "the poor chaps had been lying out there for more than seven weeks." The bodies were in a gut-wrenching state to deal with. A dreadful task to undertake as those in the burial parties were well aware that they could end up in the same state: "We got their identification discs, so there will be definite news at home for their relatives."

Rifleman Selby Grigg (LRB) tells a moving story: "Near where we were standing, a dead German who had been brought in by some of the English, was being buried and a German officer, after reading a short service in German, during which both English and Germans uncovered their heads said, 'We thank our English friends for bringing in our dead.' They stuck a bit of wood over the grave- there was no name on it only 'Vor Vaterland und Freiheit'."

Private Layton (RWR) admitted to having "mucked in and dug graves for the dead." RSM Beck (RWR) noted that "a few men of the regiment assisted in burying the dead of the Somerset Light Infantry who were killed on December 19th." A rifleman of the London Rifle Brigade helped to bury 10 dead Germans that were lying in a ditch in front of the trenches. He could have taken a pickelhaube helmet from one of them as a souvenir but "did not fancy taking it from a corpse..." Lance Corporal Coulson of the same battalion commended the Germans on being "good enough to bring in our dead out of some ruined houses by their trenches so that we could give them burial here."

Leutnant Zehmisch wrote that "my men buried fallen English and Germans whose bodies were completely dehydrated."

On New Year's Eve, Germans opposite the Royal Irish Fusiliers waved to the "Faughs" as they were known, to come over, so Captain G.V.W. Hill removed all signs of his rank and met two Germans in No Man's Land who informed him that there was a dead British soldier lying in front of their trench. He asked them to remove the identity disc and to bury the soldier. (Private Robert Boyd of the 2/ Inniskillings had lain there since 1st November and is commemorated on the Ploegsteert Memorial because his grave in the event was never discovered.)

It is doubtful that before Christmas an official plan was conceived to deal with the problems of unburied bodies. However, it was a logical development of the spontaneous meetings in No Man's Land, when decisions were taken by officers in the trenches. It was convenient that higher levels of authority were able to point to these pragmatic needs to deflect attention away from the fact that there had been a mass fraternisation with the enemy in the first place.

As the War dragged on and armistices were actively discouraged, the problems of dealing with the dead were magnified. On the Somme in 1916, for example, some of the corpses lay in No Man's Land from July until the spring of 1917, like that of poet Serjeant Will Streets, a Sheffield Pal and miner.

Dealing with burials at this stage of the War was a haphazard affair. The Red Cross played an important role in organising and collating burials with Fabian Ware an influential figure. After being rejected by the Army for being too old for active service, he commanded a mobile ambulance unit provided by the British Red Cross Society and concerned by the desperate need for an ordered organisation to deal with collecting, collating and burying bodies, he soon became the driving force behind the setting up of the Imperial War Graves Commission which was founded on a number of principles, one of which was that bodies were not to be repatriated.

We get an inkling of the development of that principle concerning an entry in the 11th Brigade War Diary for 28th December. A telegram was received by the Rifle Brigade from Lord Dunalley requesting that his son Captain Prittie be buried at home. He was killed during the attack on the19th December and buried "on the 20th instant not in a coffin and in wet ground." The diary's author concluded: "I do not recommend that this request be granted." In the course of the War very few bodies were repatriated, 60 at most out of 880,000. (Captain The Hon. Francis Reginald Dennis Prittie, son of the 4th Baron Dunalley of County Tipperary is buried in the Rifle House Cemetery, Plugstreet Wood. He was Mentioned in Despatches twice. Before the War he was Assistant Commissioner of the Uganda Boundary Commission from 1910 until 1914.)

BOXING DAY

Snow turned to sleet and the ceasefire continued. Those in the trenches still had no control over the artillery behind them. Captain Hamilton noted that "our guns opened fire on the second line trenches but not a rifle shot was fired all day. Such a relief to get one's early morning's duties done in peace and comfort." But he was still suspicious… "It all seemed strangely quiet at night and I hope they are not cooking some devilish plot." There was another delivery of Christmas mail "with stacks of good things for everybody." The officers of 'A' Company relaxed smoking "jolly good german cigars", Hamilton as usual refusing to acknowledge the enemy with a capital 'G'!

Lieutenant Drummond (RFA) who took the photograph of the Royal Warwicks and Saxons, "soon discovered that places where we were usually shot at were quite safe, and looking down towards the trenches, it was just like Earl's Court Exhibition."

Life for the 2/ Seaforth Highlanders was not so quiet and peaceful. Jim Davie wrote that "our Artillery opened fire as did theirs and brought to a close the most extraordinary proceedings I believe in the Annals of History." The Battalion Commander had probably not heard about the events of Christmas Eve and Christmas Day; but once informed he was not prepared to allow continued fraternisation on Boxing Day and thereafter, thus confirming the view of Major John Hawksley of the Royal Field Artillery, attached to the 4th Division, who considered that they were uncomfortable with a ceasefire and "would have none of it." Lieutenant Bairnsfather (RWR), who rarely missed an opportunity to socialise, dismissed the Scotsmen for "having little of it" whereas "on our right the Somersets were having some, but not as much as ourselves." So for the Seaforths the ceasefire had been broken- Jim Davie told his wife that "you will see we had not a bad Xmas at all but the funny thing is we are carrying on the same as usual looking for each other's blood again."

The Rifle Brigade's diarist recorded that "all still very quiet. Germans continue to show signs of friendliness. No sniping. There was more fraternisation, swapping of gifts and taking of photographs."

The 11th Brigade were warned that "if there should be any cessation of fire today or at any time as there was yesterday, great care should be taken that the enemy is not allowed in sight of our trenches and entanglements as he would gain valuable information."

27TH TO 30TH DECEMBER

To dampen spirits that had been temporarily raised over Christmas, it was now raining again. At least the Seaforth Highlanders were due to be relieved in the evening of 27th December and the Royal Warwicks the following day. It was still possible, according to Hamilton, to "walk about as if there were no enemy within 100 yards of us."

The ceasefire, as before, afforded the opportunity to improve trench defences. The Royal Warwicks heard the Germans doing the same. The Rifle Brigade found that hostilities "still have not been properly resumed, though finding their advances rather coldly received and not encouraged, the enemy do not walk about quite so much; but peace still reigns. We got to such terms that they sent over to warn us that hostilities were to recommence and we several times walked out to tell their patrols to keep further away instead of warning them in ruder fashion."

For the period from 20th to 31st December, the diarist for the 1/ Hampshires chose to acknowledge nothing of what occurred in No Man's Land, recording only that their main trench was flooded and listing casualties. However, the 11th Brigade Diary records on 27th that the "Hants report friendly conversation with enemy continues."

A message was sent to the Somersets' trench on the left: "Dear Camerades, I beg to inform you that it is forbidden to us to go over to you but we will remain good camerades. If we shall be forced to fire, we will fire too high. Please tell me if you are English or Irishmen. I remain yours truly, Camerade X Y. "

Serjeant Hugh Wilson (RIF) recalled that "some of the enemy came half way and beckoned us to meet them. We did not want to have anything to do with them, so long as they did not fire we would not." It was understandable that the Commanding Officers should harbour suspicious feelings: "… orders were given to keep a strict watch while on sentry duty… I saw one of our corporals go to meet them and remained talking for a while, and it was quite amusing to see the heads all along on both sides popping up to watch this affair in front. I heard a whistle sound and saw it was our CO signalling to the corporal to come back, so they parted." When the corporal returned he was placed under arrest by the CO for having communicated with the enemy. Wilson hardly put the corporal's mind at rest when asked what might happen to him. "I said 'they generally shot' people for such activity but it was only a lesson for him, for he was let off afterwards."

Private B. Hutchings (HR) recorded an interesting story: "I remember one day during the truce, they accidentally killed one of our H.Q. Signallers and they sent

Serjeant Hugh Wilson (RIF)
Royal Irish Fusiliers Museum, Armagh

over and apologised and the last day of the truce one of their fellows brought over a message to say they had orders to open fire with their automatic machines but their first shots would be fired high. Captain Unwin in return gave him a box of chocolates and they certainly acted according to the message."

The truce came to an abrupt end on 27th December for the 1/ East Lancashires. At about 9.30 a.m. a German was shot dead. In retaliation two men were wounded. The perpetrator was found to be a 16 or 17 year old lance corporal who had fired himself up with some tots of rum. Private Roe did not mince his words: "It was a wonderful achievement to shoot down a man standing behind his trench unarmed and smoking, a man that placed his trust in us." Roe and his Company were uncomfortable with the idea that the mutual agreement had been broken by them: "The honour of the British Army was at stake and we lost it."

A similar happening was observed by Harry Morgan (RWR): "A German soldier was walking along his parapet carrying a bucket when one of the members of my company further up the line, took deliberate aim and shot him. Inevitable perhaps, ordered maybe, but I felt unhappy that it was one of us that had broken the unwritten trust. The unfortunate man had no sooner hit the ground, when they hit us with everything they had, a rapid fire to exceed all previous rapid firings."

The 1/ Hampshires' truce came to an end on 28th December: "The Germans have opened fire on us, killing one and wounding two quite unexpectedly. An apology was sent in at dusk- it was only a verbal one and apparently was made to excuse the conduct of their officers who forced them to fire."

The GOC of the 4th Division expressed the hope that the Somersets, East Lancashires and Rifle Brigade were availing themselves of the opportunity to strengthen their defences. They were reminded again that they were not to allow the enemy near their defences. The 11th Brigade's GOC visited the Somersets' trenches on New Year's Eve.

The 11th Brigade War Diary is more informative, reporting "a friendly conversation with the enemy at 8.30 a.m. and a message received at 8.30 p.m. from the Germans via the Hampshires: 'Gentlemen our automatic rifle has been ordered from the Colonel to begin fire again at midnight, we take it honour to award you this fact.'" The message had been sent to Brigade Head Quarters by Captain Unwin of the Hampshires. (Captain Lancelot Urquhart Unwin was killed on 27th April during the 2nd Battle of Ypres- he has no known grave and his name is one of 54,406 to be found on the Menin Gate.)

By 7.45 p.m. on 30th December the situation was unchanged. A German biplane flying high dropped two bombs close to the East Lancashires' trenches. A message was sent with cigars, to the Somersets from the Saxons, explaining they were forbidden to visit the English but hoped to remain comrades and, if ordered to fire, would fire high.

On 30th December the Germans issued an official request for a New Year armistice to bury more dead. A document lodged in the records of the London Rifle Brigade was dated 31st December 1914 but was not translated until 16th April 1917. The proposed ceasefire was to take place between 10 a.m. and 2.00 p.m. (German time) if agreed to in writing by relevant English Commanding Officers. A boundary line would have to be agreed by German and British officers which could, in no circumstances, be crossed. All ranks of the English army were to avoid crossing the line but the dead were to be carried over by German soldiers where necessary. During the period there was to be a ceasefire to the east of Plugstreet Wood from St. Yves to Le Gheer. There was to be no artillery fire into any area behind the lines. The British officer in charge of the infantry and artillery in the sector was to declare his assent in writing and send his reply to the German officer who sent it originally. An ultimatum was issued: if the statement of agreement was not back in possession of the German officer by 8 a.m. on 31st December (German time) the truce could not be observed. The response? The 11th Brigade War Diary tersely records "Reply impossible to arrange." By this stage it was clear that British High Command had had its fill of unofficial peace initiatives- an official one was out of the question.

NEW YEAR

On New Year's Eve, Rifleman N.H. Simons (RB), aged 21, was killed probably by a sniper and is buried in Rifle House Cemetery in the Wood.

Apparently the Germans celebrated the New Year with "great vigour". On New Year's Eve, opposite the Somersets, the Germans blew trumpets, sang and hung lanterns on their barbed wire.

The Royal Warwicks and Seaforth Highlanders spent the lead up to the New Year behind the lines. Captain Hamilton's men of 'A' Company "are sending Princess Mary's gift boxes home. It is greatly appreciated. Bruce Bairnsfather dined with us, sang some of his songs, showed us some of his sketches and we all saw the New Year in." It must have been some celebration because his conclusion was… "O dear!"

FIRST DISCOVERED IN THE ALLUVIAL DEPOSITS OF SOUTHERN FLANDERS. FEEDS ALMOST EXCLUSIVELY ON JAM AND WATER BISCUITS. HOBBY: FILLING SANDBAGS, ON DARK AND RAINY NIGHTS

Bruce Bairnsfather's "Old Bill"
© 2014 Estate of Barbara Bruce Littlejohn

Bairnsfather's cartoons, or sketches as he preferred to call them, were based on his and fellow officers experiences and memories of amusing events that happened to the 'Alfs' and 'Berts' under their command, not to mention his great creation- "Old Bill, Leo Maritimus… full of plum and apple and determination." A collection of his cartoons was published by the *Bystander* magazine and proved hugely popular, selling over 200,000 copies by the end of 1916.

Armed with sore heads and hangovers, Hamilton and his subalterns marched their Companies from their billets in La Crèche back to the trenches on New Year's Day: "It poured in torrents the whole way, and we arrived drenched to the skin." The Saxons were very quiet and not for the first time he did a round of the sentries warning them to be on their guard. A typically British scene took place on 2nd January. Although the artillery was at work, there was little rifle fire. Captain Robert Hamilton records in his diary that he and some of the Royal Warwicks officers were confident and foolhardy enough to have their meals "at a table in the sunken road", just below their trenches and a mere 80 yards or so from the Germans. Typically British!

Royal Warwicks' 'A' Company would have marched down St. Yves Avenue to the T junction. Their trenches were along the embankment and the Germans' in front of the trees 80 or so yards away. The picnic would have taken place not far from the T junction in the Sunken Road! Those using St. Yves Avenue were at great risk from sniper fire as it was possible to be seen from the German trenches located in front of the line of trees. (Map VI = 4F-1)   Andrew Hamilton

If Leutnant Zehmisch and other Saxon officers had received edicts from on high to end friendly contact with the enemy, some must have disregarded them, wishing to maintain the peaceful status quo. William Tapp (RWR) was astonished when a little dog trotted over No Man's land and jumped into his trench. A message was tied round its neck. It was fussed over and the message gently removed and read out: "How are you nicey Englishmen? We are all well, please send the dog back." The dog was fed some British bully beef and refused to return to the German trenches!

Dog with a message but in this case, in German trenches, in 1917
IWM Q50649

Life was relatively peaceful with a limited amount of sniping for the first few days of 1915 at Plugstreet Wood, although the 10th Infantry Brigade War Diary's entry for 1st January mentions that "the Seaforth Highlanders on the left received about 50 shells which killed two men and wounded one."

The London Rifle Brigade received orders on 7th January 1915 from General Smith-Dorrien to the effect that "informal truces with the enemy were to cease and any officer or NCO found having initiated one would be tried by court martial."

On the same day the Somerset Light Infantry's War Diary mentions that in the afternoon "one of the enemy wished to give us a message under cover of a white flag. He was told to go back to his own lines. We did not receive the message." Pumping water from trenches was still a major occupation and the wood was described as a "morass".

The end of the Somerset Light Infantry's truce came as late as 11th January: "Sniping started again in earnest. The presumption is that 'our friendly enemy of the last fortnight has been relieved'" i.e. the Prussians for the Saxons. Frederic Coleman felt that the end of the truce was "most amusing! ... Sir John French's order was short and sharp, but very much to the point. It expressed great displeasure at such carryings on."

Prowse Point Cemetery, where 16 Royal Dublin Fusiliers and 10 Royal Warwicks are buried   *Andrew Hamilton*

REACTIONS

One of the main talking points in the trenches over Christmas must have focused on how the "Top Brass" would react to what Private Layton (RWR) described neatly as "an armistice without permission." Another Private in the Regiment, Alfred Day realistically predicted that "the truce could not last any longer." Was he referring to Captain Hamilton when he suggested that if it did continue "our officer will get into trouble"?

Private William Tapp (RWR) expressed his concern on Boxing Day: "I don't know what our General would say if he knew about it" and Hamilton on the same day wrote in his trench diary "I am told the General and his staff are furious but powerless to stop it." For whatever reason, he chose to omit this comment from the final typed version of his diary but he was correct- General Smith-Dorrien of 2nd Army was indeed livid at what had taken place. It would appear he visited two sections of the trenches on Boxing Day- and was unimpressed by what he saw. It is unlikely to have been any in the Plugstreet area as it would have been mentioned in diary accounts and letters.

Smith-Dorrien was struck during his visit to trenches in another sector by the "apathy" that prevailed; some of his concerns and criticisms would have applied to sections of the 10th and 11th Brigades' trenches. He considered they were too wide, head cover was lacking in fire and communication trenches, boxes especially made by the Royal Engineers had not been used to place in the bottom of waterlogged trenches, there was a large gap in the line, there was a lack of support trenches and little had been done to dig trenches for offence. Casualties caused by sniper fire and the wet weather which resulted in "trench foot", could be "vastly" reduced he argued with proper "supervision and energy". He was critical of the narrowness of the loopholes particularly as new frames were "the easiest things in the world to make… when the loophole is so small as to ensure the safety of the enemy if he attacks, it reduces war to a farce." He left the Generals under his command in no doubt as to his feelings- they were to "keep sufficiently in touch with the state of affairs to make quite sure that what I saw in the areas I visited is not happening in other areas." He threatened to make unannounced visits as he considered them necessary.

Smith-Dorrien does not mince his words about the Christmas Truce in the final two paragraphs of his Memorandum of 27th December 1914: "I would add that, on my return, I was shown a report from one section of how, on Christmas Day, a friendly gathering had taken place of Germans and British on the neutral ground between the lines, recounting that many officers had taken part in it. This is only illustrative of the apathetic state we are gradually sinking into, apart also from illustrating that any orders I issue on the subject are useless, for I have issued the strictest orders that on no account is intercourse to be allowed between the opposing troops. To finish this war quickly, we must keep up the fighting spirit and do all we can to discourage friendly intercourse.

I am calling for particulars as to names of officers and units who took part in this Christmas gathering, with a view to disciplinary action."

The 10th and 11th Brigade's Brigadier Generals Hull and Hunter-Weston were not as forthright in their views as Smith-Dorrien but Hunter-Weston did visit the Somersets' trenches, houses and farms on New Year's Eve, making a long and very careful inspection throughout and concluded his visit by making many suggestions for improvements.

Somerset Light Infantry in their trenches- note how the soldier at the far end of the trench is ducking down for safety   South West Heritage Trust

Several front line officers must have had their cards marked, particularly those of the rank of Captain in the battalions that fraternised. Had Smith-Dorrien instituted proceedings against them all, he would have been seriously short of officers in the trenches. What Captain Hamilton, Lieutenants Cave, Black and Bairnsfather had initiated and participated in, was likely to show up in red on their records…

Hints of what the General was complaining about can be seen in Captain Hamilton's diary entries for 8th, 12th and 16th December. On 8th December: "The trenches were in the most deplorable condition. Everyone was over the ankles in liquid mud, and the communication trenches over the knees. Most of the dug outs had fallen in." Four days later it was "still raining…The Jack Johnson (German shell) coal box holes are like young lakes. … Dubs relieved us at 6.30 p.m. and we implored them to try and do something to the trenches and dugouts when it stopped raining."   On 16th December he returned to the trenches complaining bitterly again that "these dirty

Opposite page, clockwise from top left:
- *Sir John French GOC B.E.F. - National Portrait Gallery   NPG X137270*
- *General Sir Horace Smith-Dorrien GOC II Corps, promoted to GOC 2nd Army on Christmas Day 1914*
- *Lieutenant General Sir William Pulteney GOC III Corps*
- *Major General Henry Wilson GOC 4th Division - by Sir William Orpen, National Portrait Gallery   NPG 4183*
- *Brigadier General Charles Hull GOC 10th Brigade*
- *Brigadier General Aylmer Hunter-Weston 11th Brigade*

Dublin Fusiliers have done nothing but pull down anything of wood to burn." Is he referring here to the Royal Engineers' carefully constructed wooden boxes? He reported that a certain portion of the trench was waist high but with a 'stiff upper lip' he was resigned to the state of things so "… no matter we occupied it."

He must have hoped that the General's angry finger of blame be aimed at the Royal Dublin Fusiliers!

Private Latham (LRB) claimed that no disciplinary action was taken by H.Q. and at any rate no divisional orders or rebukes of any sort filtered down to the rank and file.

Hamilton's action on 30th December may have been a result of the Smith-Dorrien memorandum: in his trench diary

The New Submarine Danger
" They'll be torpedoin' us if we stick 'ere much longer, Bill "

Bruce Bairnsfather's take on the mud and flooded trenches
© *2014 Estate of Barbara Bruce Littlejohn*

he wrote: "Before marching off, I had to address the Company on their behaviour lately. In spite of my giving them more liberty and many more privileges than any other Company, there were no less than nine cases of either drunkenness or absence. I warned them all beforehand and now they will have to suffer for it." As the New Year approached, it was clearly time for the men to buckle down and forget the excesses of the Christmas period.

Lieutenant General Sir William Pulteney, Commanding Officer of III Corps, issued the following order on 2nd January 1915: "Informal understandings with the enemy are strictly forbidden. Any officer or non-commissioned officer proved to be responsible for initiating such understandings or acquiescing in any such understanding proposed by the enemy will be tried by court-martial. Commanding officers are held responsible that all officers and non-commissioned officers in their units are made acquainted with this order." The wording of the order is not dissimilar to that issued on 26th December by General Smith-Dorrien who, as of Boxing Day, had become Pulteney's new master.

The reaction of most Tommies in the trenches was one of incredulity. For Private Fairs (LRB) it was "an experience for me and I was glad to have been in the firing line and to see a real live German and talk to him." Other reactions include:

- A very merry Xmas and a most extraordinary one…
  Captain Robert Hamilton (RWR)

- There had not been an atom of hate shown by either side… There was a mutual trust about everything… The spirit of Christmas had been too much for war! … Lieutenant Bruce Bairnsfather   (Machine-Gun officer with the RWR)

- …the whole affair, I must confess, seemed and felt very touching indeed…
  Private John Mackay (SH)

- What a strange Christmas it was! … Lance Corporal J.S. Calder (LRB)

- It was so exciting… to be above the trenches in daylight- at ordinary times it meant sudden death…
  David Lloyd-Burch (10th Field Ambulance, attached to 4th Division)

- I am sorry we were relieved; it must have been a marvellous sight… Christmas will, I believe, live in history as one of the most remarkable incidents of the war… Lance Corporal Coulson (LRB)

- Altogether it is an extraordinary situation… Lieutenant Guy Cave (RWR)

- Marvellous isn't it? … Henry Williamson (LRB)

- Dear Aunt, it is hardly credible but believe me it is so. It was a sight to see enemies conversing, smiling and joking… Private Alfred Smith (RWR)

- This is an extraordinary state of things, and I don't altogether approve. Still it gives me and my observation post a quiet time…
  Major John Hawksley (RFA, attached 10th Brigade)

- It was a memorable Christmas Day in our trenches…
  Private in the London Rifle Brigade

- I would not have missed Christmas Eve for anything… It was very different to other Christmas Days I had spent especially the one in 1910 when I stood under the mistletoe with the girl I later married… Private William Tapp (RWR)

- This fantastic situation… it is quite amusing to think that a few hours ago, they were at one another's throats… Arthur Cook (SLI)

- The folk at home will not believe it but it is true… Private Colin Munro (SH)

- … how quiet and unreal it was, not to have to keep our heads low and to be walking upright in the trenches… Serjeant Hugh Wilson (machine-gunner RIF)

- It seemed like a dream… Rifleman J. Reading (RB)

- Anyone that did not see it would not believe that such a thing could happen in warfare; nevertheless it's true… Private A. Barnett (RWR)

- An enjoyable day… Corporal Samuel Judd (RWR)

- We sensed a strange quietness… Serjeant J. Philpotts (RWR)

- We spent a wonderful Christmas… Private William Setchfield (RWR)

German reactions:

- So after all, the Christmas festival, the festival of love, caused the hated enemies to be friends for a short time. I will never forget this Christmas! Leutnant Kurt Zehmisch (134th Saxon Regiment)

- In contrast another German reacted rather differently. Although he did not witness the fraternisations at Christmas, he was unimpressed when he heard that some of his unit, the 16th Bavarian Reserve Infantry Regiment, had met British soldiers of the 5th Division west of Messines. He is reported to have said that "something like this should not even be up for discussion during wartime." The identity of the German soldier? Gefreiter Adolf Hitler, whose unit H.Q. was situated at a farm called "Bethlehem"

Plugstreet Wood in winter- "There was a cloudless sky and snow lay on the ground- just the sort of day for Peace to be declared." Lieutenant Bruce Bairnsfather   J Kerr

Official Reactions

4th DIVISION:

> Fine clear cold day- frost continued. Christmas Day was celebrated in the usual fashion but there was no champagne at Division H.Q. As regards the firing line, a sort of truce was automatically established which led to the exchange of sundry courtiesies (sic) absolutely unauthorised. Xmas greetings were exchanged but are not recorded.

10th BRIGADE:

> A quiet day. No firing. The Germans appear to think that an armistice exits for Christmas Day. An informal interchange of courtesies took place between the troops in the fire trenches of both belligerents. Some valuable information was gleaned during the intercourse. The trenches seem fairly strongly held, the enemy cheerful and well fed.

1/ Royal Warwicks:

> A local truce. British and Germans intermingle between the trenches. Dead in front of trenches buried. No shot fired all day. No casualties.

2/ Seaforth Highlanders:

> Nothing to report. Hard frost and misty. Not a shot fired and we were able to walk about in the open even after the mist rose. Some trouble in keeping the Germans away from our lines .

> A sort of armistice exists and we have buried some Germans and they have buried British of the Hampshire Regiment and Germans opposite us, the 19th Saxons, 134th Regiment. Work has consisted in putting up new wire and improving trenches. Wiring operations will be continued.

2/ Royal Dublin Fusiliers: (in billets at Nieppe in France)
> No sniping or shelling heard.

1/ Royal Irish Fusiliers: (in billets at La Crèche in France))
> Beautiful frosty morning. Services for C of E and RC's in the morning. CO rode round billets to visit men at their dinners which, thanks to many kind friends at home, were good. The Christmas cards sent by the King and Queen were distributed, also Princess Mary's gifts. The officers dined together in the evening.

11th BRIGADE:

> After a night entirely free from sniping, a period of informal truce took place all day. The Germans were not allowed near our lines, met our men between the lines in most friendly terms, cigars, cigarettes, and news being exchanged freely.

1/ East Lancashire:

> All quiet, no shots fired at all.

1/ Hampshire:

> During this period nothing of interest happened.

London Rifle Brigade (attached):

> Freezing, very quiet day, practically no shooting.

1/ Somerset Light Infantry:

> There was much singing in the trenches last night by both sides. The Germans informed us that they had captured a wounded officer (this was thought to be Lieutenant K.G.G. Dennys who commanded one of the attacking platoons of 'B' Company on the 19th.) There was a sharp frost last night which continued during the day and the weather was very seasonable. Not a shot or shell was fired by either side in our neighbourhood; and both sides walked about outside their trenches unconcernedly. It afforded a good opportunity for inspecting our trenches by daylight. The enemy's works were noted to be very strong. A very peaceful day.

1/ Rifle Brigade:

> Everything extraordinarily quiet. Germans came out of their trenches and met our people half way; all friendly and helped collect each other's dead; no shooting.

CONCLUSION

The Christmas Truce and the fraternisations in No Man's Land were a spontaneous reaction by both sides to a shocking month of poor weather, flooded trenches, sniping and the British attack on 19th December which caused deaths not only of Germans but also of British troops. It was Fritz and Tommy, the "other ranks", who started the cross-trench Christmas greetings, the singing and invitations to meet in between the lines. The majority of their Company Commanders were prepared to allow initial meetings on Christmas Eve and the widespread encounters on Christmas Day. For some officers, toleration was an easier option than attempting to herd hundreds of men back to their trenches.

Royal Irish Fusilier de-lousing in a trench
Royal Irish Fusiliers Museum, Armagh

"Top Brass" reaction was predictable: threats of court martial were issued about future similar occurrences. It was tacitly understood that the somewhat subversive and unmilitary decisions taken by officers could not be punished- too many had been involved. In seeking to defend and justify what had happened, the chance to collect and bury bodies was emphasised but it is unlikely that a blind eye was turned in order to facilitate this- news of the truces reached Brigade, Division and Corps Head Quarters generally after the incidents had transpired.

We have been struck, during our research, by the appalling conditions endured by the troops of both sides in the Plugstreet trenches. Much is made of Passchendaele in 1917, but at Plugstreet, the state of trenches, No Man's Land, tracks, roads and pathways in December 1914 were on a par. Corporal Arthur Cook (SLI) spoke eloquently for those who had to suffer: "It had been a very hard winter and the hardships we had to endure are indescribable, the mud and fleas, rather lice, were one of the worst discomforts, the mud we had to plough through in the wood was two to three feet deep, it was easy for a man to fall down in the dark and disappear in the mud and never be seen alive again."

Censorship of soldiers' letters was an accepted part of life at the Front. So how was it that by early January 1915, newspapers throughout the country were publishing letters about the truce? How was this possible? In general, officers of the rank of Captain and below censored their men's letters, a task that most found an irritant. Raymond Asquith, the Prime Minister's son who was in the 3/ Grenadier Guards, found it a laborious chore in 1915 reading through "very long and dull letters." Geoffrey Donaldson, a 22 year old Captain of the Territorial 1/ 7 Royal Warwicks found it irksome in 1916 trawling through stacks of his men's letters and "such a waste of time censoring them as there is scarcely nothing to cross out." Letters to be censored after Christmas 1914, however, would have contained plenty to cross out but in many instances they remained as originally written. The censors had experienced the "unbelievable" and "unique" fraternisations themselves; they were, perhaps, unwilling to censor material that was so dear to their men's hearts and that they were so eager to share with their families at home.

In a remarkably thoughtful and poignant piece, Private Roe (ELR)) maintained that "the awful slaughter had been unable to check the spirit of Christmas. On Christmas Eve something 'went west'. Would friendliness happen again at Christmas? Would ambitious Statesmen and Warlords, who only think of the Regimental officer and common soldier in terms of mathematics, cast aside their ambitions, stupidity, pride and hatred and allow the angel of peace, instead of the angel of death, to spread his wings over stricken and bleeding humanity. I, or any of my comrades, as far as I can ascertain, bear no malice or hatred against the German soldier. He has got to do as he is told, and so have we.' Roe admitted that he was "a damn bad soldier" for preaching peace in the spirit of Christmas.

The editor of the *Carlisle Journal* wrote on Tuesday 5th January 1915 about how the War was briefly humanised: "Amid the welter of bloodshed, bitterness and hatred in to which Germany has plunged Europe, it is some slight consolation to read in the letters of British soldiers at the front accounts of the humanising influence of Christmas on the combatants in the trenches. The Germans in this campaign have shown such a contempt not merely for chivalry but even for the rules of war as understood by civilised races that it is refreshing to find that among the private soldiers at all events the better instincts have not altogether been crushed by the horrors that have been perpetrated. Many accounts have been published of the strange and unexpected fraternising which took place between the British and Germans on Christmas Day."

Harold Lewis of the Royal Field Artillery was stationed in Britain when the Christmas Truce occurred. He was sceptical that it had actually happened: "Although it would be arrogant to say that the thing didn't take place, I very much doubt whether anything of the nature or the magnitude that have been claimed for it took place at all. And particularly because the two armies concerned, the German with that rigid discipline and our own with the finest discipline of a fighting force there was, are not likely to break that tradition. And if anybody tried, what were the NCOs doing? What were the officers doing? I think the whole thing borders on the fairy tale and may be classed with the Russians with snow on their boots and the 'Angel of Mons'." (A rumour had been sweeping the country that Russian troops had landed in Scotland to help their British ally and some had been seen in Edinburgh "with snow on their boots"! "The Angel of Mons" was a popular legend about a group of angels who purportedly protected members of the British Army during the Battle of Mons.) Harold Lewis was not alone in doubting that the Christmas Truce happened- a reading of this book, does we hope, extinguish such scepticism!

It is indeed humbling to think that I have a direct link to an extraordinary event which is sure to provoke a huge amount of interest in its centenary year and beyond. But when placed in the context of the Great War, the Christmas Truce was arguably little more than an insignificant blip during the most inhumane and destructive of wars. Described by my grandfather Captain Robert Hamilton and emphasised in capital letters in his trench diary as "A DAY UNIQUE IN THE HISTORY OF THE WORLD", the Christmas Truce must be one of the most famous of historical events to have had so little effect. It was a short one-off moment when man's innate "goodness" overcame his ability to press the self-destruct button. The "War to end all Wars"? Only 21 years later, after enduring and surviving the War, his diary entry for 24th August 1939 was a depressing appraisal of the situation: "The War news is hopeless- I do not see what is to prevent another European War." There was about to be another "suicide of Europe" as Pope Benedict XV had labelled the first few months of the Great War in 1914.

Lieutenant Bruce Bairnsfather asserted that the Christmas Truce had "put a little human punctuation mark in our lives of cold and humid hate." It was only a tiny full stop in the burgeoning and depressing text of four years of man's senseless inhumanity.

Appendices

I SOME OF THOSE WHO PARTICIPATED:

Captain Robert Hamilton, 1/ Royal Warwicks:

The Hamilton family originated from Silverton Hill in Hamilton, Lanarkshire. In the early 1800s the family moved to Tiddington near Stratford-on-Avon where Robert was born in 1877. He was sent to Trinity College, Glenalmond which he attended from 1892 to 1896. He was a fine all-round sportsman excelling in cricket, rugby, tennis, gymnastics and fives.

Glenalmond was chosen to prepare him for a career in the Indian Civil Service or the Army; his grandfather Sir Robert had been an influential

Captain Robert Hamilton, 1/ Royal Warwicks
Andrew Hamilton

member of the Raj in India, playing an important role during the Indian Mutiny of 1857 for which he received a formal Vote of Thanks from both Houses of Parliament and his father Frederic had been in the Army. Robert was placed in the College's Army Class stream; he enjoyed training exercises and route marches in the Scottish countryside and decided he preferred the greater excitement and physical challenges that the Army offered than those of a desk-bound career.

On leaving Glenalmond, he joined the Norfolk Regiment with whom he fought in the Boer War, for which he received the Queen's and King's medals. The Norfolks remained in Bloemfontein until 1906 when they were posted to Bombay (Mumbai) early in 1907, during which time Robert reached the rank of full Lieutenant.

Before the outbreak of the Great War, Robert was on the 'reserve' list, living in Sourton, Devon with his wife Irene and their children Cynthia and Richard. They had married in St. James's Church at Walton Hall, the home of his father-in-law Sir Charles Mordaunt and family.

When the British Expeditionary Force was mobilised in the summer of 1914, Robert had been transferred to the 1/ Royal Warwicks and took part in their campaigns through the Marne and Aisne during the autumn. He was promoted to captain on 16th September. He kept a diary of his experiences which are the focus of *Meet at Dawn, Unarmed* by Andrew Hamilton and Alan Reed, published in 2009.

He returned to England on 12th January, his first leave for over six months. He had suffered problems with his ears for many years, a condition that worsened due to shellfire and the cold and damp; he was posted to the Hereford Detention Barracks which he commanded until the end of the War. Having spent six months at the Front 'doing his bit' he found dealing with the Conscientious Objectors there a major challenge. He announced the end of the War to the delirious townsfolk of Hereford and organised the military procession to the cathedral on Sunday 17th November 1918.

After the War he retired from the Army and returned to farming in Devon, becoming 8th Baronet on the death of his father in 1921. He rarely talked about his experiences in 1914 but his diary for 1914 provides a detailed account of the important first months of mobile warfare, the beginnings of trench warfare and, of course, the Christmas Truce and his role in it.

There is an interesting point to be made about his career; many of his fellow officers were Mentioned in Despatches by Brigadier General Hull in early January 1915. Letters from officers like Lieutenant Guy Cave and his batman Private Sperry suggest that he was highly respected. Sperry wrote to Renie Hamilton from his hospital bed in Aberdeen wishing her husband a "Merry Christmas" and a safe return home "for if ever there was a man that deserved a welcome home it is dear old Captain Hamilton. He is loved by every man in the regiment, he tries to make every man happy like himself and I am longing for the time to come that I can grip him by the hand and have a chat like old times again." Mere speculation but one wonders whether initiation of a Christmas Truce in his area of the Plugstreet Wood sector had counted against him…

Robert's Army career ended after the War but a good friend of his in the early days of training and campaigns from late August to mid-October was the younger Bernard Law Montgomery, the future Field Marshal, who was wounded during the Battle of Méteren on 13th October 1914 and returned to England for the treatment of his wounds. How would his career have fared if he had been an instigator of the Christmas truce? Would he have reigned in his superiors like Hamilton or would he have "gone with the flow" and maybe had his card marked?

Lieutenant Guy Cave, 1/ Royal Warwicks:

Guy Cave was born in 1885 in Tunbridge Wells, the third son of William John Cave J.P. He went to Tonbridge School where he was in the Rugby XV and Rowing eight, after which he worked for the family firm of Cave and Benoist who traded in fabrics. He was sent to France to learn the language and to familiarise himself with French manufacturing techniques.

Lieutenant Guy Cave, 1/ Royal Warwicks
David Cave

The publication of *Meet at Dawn, Unarmed* by Andrew Hamilton and Alan Reed about the 1/ Royal Warwicks in 1914 provided a pleasant surprise for his family for whom Guy's life has been shrouded in mystery. After the War, he lost close connection with his four brothers as a result of an incident when he had issued threats with a gun in the family's business office. His nephew David Cave is of the opinion that his uncle was aggrieved at having been replaced in the family firm by a younger brother who had not "done his bit" during the War.

After the excitements of the Christmas Truce, hostilities escalated in 1915 and the 2nd Battle of Ypres was a tragic time for the 1/ Royal Warwicks- many of the Battalion's 500 names on the Menin Gate of those without a known grave, were killed in that battle. Guy was hospitalised along with Bruce Bairnsfather, both suffering from shell shock and it is possible Guy suffered from the effects of the German gas attacks on 25th April. Once recovered, he served in Ireland and after the War, he worked for Crosse and Blackwell as a salesman.

Cave joined Captain Hamilton's 'A' Company on 4th November from 6/ Royal Fusiliers when the Royal Warwicks were based near Armentières. He was welcomed by Hamilton and became one of the senior officer's 'Black Hat Gang' of junior officers or subalterns, whom he described as some of "the deepest drinkers and worst behaved of characters (in peacetime) in the Company." Cave was a lively character who fitted in well, Hamilton noting that they "celebrated the end of their time in Armentières in good old English style and enjoyed ourselves very much" helped along no doubt by the odd 'Bottle of the Boy'! (Bollinger champagne)

Guy clearly enjoyed life behind the lines. Just before Christmas, Hamilton and Cave went round to see the Plover girls in Steenwerck and "of course young Guy must needs lose his heart to the elder one, because she could sing and dance." On 2nd January Hamilton and his subalterns had their meals "at a table placed in the sunken road" with the Germans 80 yards away. The Germans could well have heard the laughter caused by Cave recounting "his numerous love affairs", just as Major Poole, the Battalion's Commanding Officer, turned up for an inspection.

Hamilton was well respected- Guy Cave reported that he and his Company's captain "get on very well together. He is a very good fellow." The young subaltern's language skills were much appreciated- Cave "speaks the language like a native." Guy understood the importance of his command of French: "I must tell you" he wrote in an 'all- round' letter to family and friends on 27th October 1914, "the language is an enormous asset… it was just good knowledge of the language and the people that allowed me to make things that would have been uncomfortable, quite comfortable. The French are for the most part inclined to bleed Tommy i.e. to make him pay through the nose for everything." Cave was also given the role of interrogating locals suspected of spying for the Germans.

He wrote an interesting description of the Christmas Truce although he seems to have played exactly the same role as Captain Hamilton in the unfolding drama! It is out of the question that he would have been in a position to sanction a Private to go into No Man's Land. No doubt his readers were suitably impressed… In a letter to his younger brother Jack, Guy thanked him for sending out a copy of *The Tatler*, one assumes the same one mentioned by Hamilton in his description of Christmas Day: "The Black Hat gang had rigged up an enormous dug out and had plastered the walls with Tatler pictures of all the girls."

Life for Guy Cave after the War was a sad one. Affected by shell shock, divorced by his wife with the subsequent loss of contact with his children, he died of lung cancer in the Clarence Nursing home in Tunbridge Wells at the comparatively early age of 63. His Christmas at Plugstreet Wood must have been one of the few memorable moments of his later years.

Serjeant A.H. Cook, 1/ Somerset Light Infantry:

Arthur Cook was one of a small and illustrious band of British soldiers who survived front line action from 22nd August 1914 right through to 11th November 1918 and was the only one in the Somerset Light Infantry to do so.

Arthur Cook was born on 22nd November 1888 into a large family in the village of Wroughton near Swindon. The Cooks were poor but the children were brought up according to sound Christian principles. Arthur was a talented musician; he played the piano, organ and trombone, as well as singing baritone in the church choir. Faced by unemployment, Arthur enlisted with the Somerset Light Infantry at Taunton in November 1910, the first of his family to do so and without his parents' blessing. He was desperate to join up but was too small physically so he lied about his age, claiming to be younger than he was to gain acceptance, "a lapse" as he described it that he never regretted: "It gave me a home in the finest regiment in the Army." During the first years of his service, his musical skills came to the fore in the regimental band.

When War broke out, he was a Lance Corporal but by 1915 he had been promoted to Serjeant and to Colour Serjeant in 1916 after his efforts on the disastrous first day of the Battle of the Somme on 1st July. He commanded what was left of his platoon that had not been gunned down in the Germans' second line which they had withdrawn to but such was the ferocity of the Germans' defence that he had to order his men back to the Germans' front line. They held their ground in a fierce grenade fight until late in the evening at which point he and other survivors were forced to retreat. Casualties on that fateful day included 26 officers and 438 other ranks.

"Beefeater" Arthur Cook
South West Heritage Trust

Arthur Cook was wounded just nine days before the Armistice was signed on 11th November and was sent to York Military Hospital to recuperate. He received the Distinguished Conduct Medal for his actions during the Battle of the Selle: "During the advance on Preseau, on 1st November 1918, the line was held up by the heavy fire from two machine-gun posts. He organised a small party and rushed them one after another, killing the teams, and capturing the guns. He then returned to his company, re-organised them and led them on to their final objective. He set a splendid example throughout of courage and good leadership."

Cook was highly regarded and on Armistice Day in 1920 was selected to represent the Somerset Light Infantry at the funeral of the Unknown Soldier in Westminster Abbey. He served with the 2nd Battalion in India and in 1926 at Khartoum. In 1928 he was chosen as one of the few "Old Contemptibles" who had fought throughout the War, to represent the Regiment again at the opening of the spectacular memorial for those who died during the campaign on the Aisne at La Ferté-sous-Jouarre (designed by George Goldsmith and unveiled by Lieutenant General Sir William Pulteney).

In 1932 he was discharged from the Army after 22 years' service and in 1934 applied for and was accepted as a "Beefeater" at the Tower of London. Within just nine years he had been promoted to the highest rank of Chief Warder, a post he held until retirement in 1954. He died two years later in Hastings after a major operation.

Arthur Cook had a remarkable career during which he received 11 medals and decorations and was in great demand as the "voice" of the Great War's B.E.F. making frequent appearances on T.V. and radio. One of his great regrets was his failure to find a publisher for his detailed and perceptive account of his experiences of the Great War.

Lieutenant Bruce Bairnsfather, Machine-Gun officer in 1/ Royal Warwicks:

On 31st December Captain Robert Hamilton recorded in his diary that "Bruce Bairnsfather dined with us and showed us some of his sketches." His fellow officers in the *estaminet* would have been chortling at some of the cartoons depicting humorous moments they had shared and the trials and tribulations of the Tommies under their command, 'Old Bill', 'Alfs' and 'Berts'. These were no doubt the 'prototypes' of cartoons that within two years would make Bairnsfather a household name- a collection of his cartoons in *Fragments from France* published by the *Bystander* had sold 200,000 copies by 1916. So many of the aspects of life in the trenches experienced by the 1/ Royal Warwicks from 20th November, when Bairnsfather joined the battalion as a machine-gun officer, feature in his work- the flooded trenches, the dangers and discomforts, the monotony of the rations, the shelled buildings, and the strange happenings in No Man's Land over Christmas to name but a few. And of course, the characters, the Tommies, whose antics amused him, Hamilton and others.

He was born into an Army family in 1887 at Murree in India (now the Pakistani Punjab) where his father was stationed. His parents were artistic, his mother a painter and his father a musician and composer. From an early age Bruce loved to draw and when only eight, his ability to draw and poke fun at people and situations was clear. He was sent to the United Services College at Westward Ho! and the family moved to Bishopton just outside Stratford-on-Avon in 1904.

When he left school he joined the Cheshires, his father's old Regiment, despite failing his Sandhurst entrance exams but resigned in 1907. He continued a link with the Army by joining the 3rd Warwickshire Militia; his heart, though, was set on being an artist and reluctantly his father allowed him to attend the John Hassall   **93**

Bruce Bairnsfather enjoying his favourite cigarette, a Gold Flake at Christmas 1914 in front of a shell crater at St. Yves
© 2014 Estate of Barbara Bruce Littlejohn

School of Art in London, after which he struggled to find his niche- he joined the Old Memorial Theatre at Stratford-on-Avon as an electrical engineer and his lucky break came when he met the novelist Marie Corelli who lived in the town; she introduced him to Thomas Lipton the tea magnate who opened the relevant doors for Bruce to design advertising sketches for famous brands like Keen's Mustard, Player's Cigarettes and, of course, Lipton's Tea.

Bairnsfather joined the Royal Warwicks on 12th September 1914. As he had received military training with the Militia, he was fast-tracked at the Front, arriving in Armentières on 20th November as a Second Lieutenant in charge of a machine-gun section which consisted of two teams of six men in each. After the excitements of the Christmas Truce, he was hospitalised, suffering from shell shock after the 2nd Battle of Ypres on 25 April 1915. He was appointed "Officer Cartoonist" by the War Office on his recovery and toured France and Italy raising troop morale. Still in contact when at the Hereford Detention Barracks, Captain Robert Hamilton made a note in his diary for 24th September 1916 that his friend Bruce "had been given a pass anywhere on the French and Italian Front."

A major "Old Bill" industry blossomed after the War- he featured on mugs, plates, cups and jigsaw puzzles. Bairnsfather wrote books, plays, musicals and films. He was overlooked in World War II by the British Establishment but due to contacts made when he lived in America between 1916 and 1932, he was appointed official cartoonist for the American Forces in Europe. Thereafter he was beset by marital and financial problems and died of cancer in 1959.

Bruce Bairnsfather's "Old Bill" and "Alfs" and "Berts" did much to raise morale of troops fighting in Europe in the Great War. The Generals and the Establishment were disdainful of his work- *The Times* criticized his drawings for depicting a "degraded type of face" and the Imperial War Museum considered there was insufficient artistic merit in his work to warrant inclusion in their War Art galleries. One can only hope that such an attitude will soften and that one of Britain's finest cartoonists will find a space on the Museum's walls. He was, after all, much loved by the men in the trenches- their lives were seriously humour-free so Bairnsfather cartoons were always eagerly awaited. A 22 year old Cambridge botany student, Captain Geoffrey Donaldson, who volunteered for action and was subsequently killed on the Somme in July 1916, sang the praises of Bruce Bairnsfather's work in a letter to his mother written a month before his death: "There is a second volume of Bairnsfather sketches out which are really excellent for they have caught the atmosphere of the trenches exactly… like the Bible and Shakespeare they should be on every bookshelf" and 100 years after their first outings in the *estaminets* and billets frequented by the 1/ Royal Warwicks in late 1914 and early 1915, they deserve to be savoured, suitably acknowledged and celebrated.

Le Café de la Gare at Steenwerck.   Musée de la Vie Rurale de Steenwerck

Bruce Bairnsfather and fellow officers of the 1/ Royal Warwicks enjoyed life to the full, highlighted by Captain Hamilton's diary entry for 6th January 1915: "We all met at the station Estaminet, and had a most magnificent dinner, and many songs after. Guy Cave said he would see if he could round up some ladies for a hop, and produced four. The fun was fast and furious, and so was the dancing till the proprietor announced it was time we took the ladies home. Young Bruce was quite in his element."

II THE CEMETERIES AND THE MEMORIAL IN THE PLUGSTREET AREA

Burials and Commemorations of the 10th and 11th Brigades in December 1914.

CEMETERIES / MEMORIAL			
Lancashire Cottage	East Lancashires	6	
	Hampshire	29	(13 on 19th December)
	London Rifle Brigade	4	
London Rifle Brigade	East Lancashires	1	(on Christmas Day Pte. J. Finnigan)
	Rifle Brigade	2	
	Royal Dublin Fusiliers	1	(Pte. John Cashman, 19, probably died of wounds, on Christmas Day)
	Royal Warwicks	1	
	Somerset Light Infantry	1	
Ploegsteert Churchyard	Hampshire	1	(Major G.H. Parker, aged 44, on 19th December)
Ploegsteert Memorial	Hampshire	2	(both on 19th December)
	Rifle Brigade	9	(3 on 19th December)
	Royal Irish Fusiliers	4	
	Royal Warwicks	4	
	Seaforth Highlanders	4	
	Somerset Light Infantry	13	(5 on 19th December)
Ploegsteert Wood Military	London Rifle Brigade	1	(singer Arthur Bassingham on Christmas night)
	Somerset Light Infantry	28	(26 on 19th December including 3 Captains)
Prowse Point	Royal Dublin Fusiliers	16	(2 on Christmas Eve)
	Royal Warwicks	10	
Rifle House	London Rifle Brigade	2	(one on 19th December)
	Rifle Brigade	29	(including 24 on 19th December including 2 Captains)

Strand Military	Rifle Brigade	4	
	Royal Engineers (attached)	1	
	Somerset Light Infantry	4	(3 on 19th December)
	Total	**177**	(78 on 19th December)

The original Somerset Light Infantry plot of 32 graves in what is now Ploegsteert Wood Military Cemetery (Map VI = 5D-1) South West Heritage Trust

Tombes de Guerre du Commonwealth
Commonwealth War Graves
Oorlogsgraven van het Gemenebest

Prowse Point
Military Cemetery

Mud Corner
Cemetery

Toronto Avenue
Cemetery

Ploegsteert Wood
Military Cemetery

Rifle House
Cemetery

From top left clockwise:
• CWGC signs for Plugstreet Wood cemeteries
• The sneering lion at Ploegsteert Memorial
• The Ploegsteert Memorial

III
A Tour of the Cemeteries of Plugstreet Wood

A tour of the cemeteries in and around Plugstreet Wood combines a pleasant walk with a rewarding experience. Refer to Map VI on page 104 for grid references and we recommend the 1/ 10,000 map, the most detailed map of the area- IGN, Carte Topographique de Belgique, Mesen (Messines), 28/ 6 Sud.

We suggest you start the tour after refreshments at the excellent "Auberge" (5B-1) which is on the Ploegsteert to Messines road where you can leave your car with the owner's permission. To gain an overall view of Plugstreet Wood and the events leading up to and including the truce, it is worth starting with a visit to the Plugstreet Experience 14-18 museum which is across the road from "L' Auberge".

Turn left out of the museum and walk to "Hyde Park Corner" (5B-1). Explore the superb Ploegsteert Memorial. It was unveiled by the Duke of Brabant on 7th June 1931. The panels list the names of over 11,000 soldiers who have no known graves and who died in a large area surrounding Ploegsteert in Belgium and across the border in France. The Memorial is surrounded by the Berks Cemetery Extension (876 burials) and across the road is Hyde Park Corner (Royal Berks) Cemetery (87 burials including four Germans) which was begun in April 1915 and contains two famous graves- of Ronnie Poulton Palmer the England Rugby captain in 1914 and a 16 year old boy soldier, Albert French who lied about his age to get to the Front. The Memorial and two cemeteries were designed by Harold Chalton Bradshaw. The lions, one sneering, the other smiling, guard the memorial and were sculpted by Gilbert Ledward.

Walking north, take the first path on your right, "Mud Lane" (5B) which was used by the troops marching to and from St Yves. After about a kilometre, you will reach "Mud Corner" (4D-2). Designed by G.H. Goldsmith, the cemetery was begun in June 1917 during the Battle of Messines and contains 85 graves of Australians and New Zealanders. Continue a further 400 metres, turn left and you will reach Prowse Point Cemetery (4D-1), the only one in Belgium named after an individual, Major Charles Prowse (CO of 1/SLI) who made a stand here in October 1914. On the first day of the Battle of the Somme, the fateful 1st July 1916, he was killed when in charge of 11th Brigade. The cemetery was started by the Royal Dublin Fusiliers and the Royal Warwicks in November 1914. It was designed by W.H. Cowlishaw and contains 225 graves; of those killed in December 1914 there were 10 Royal Warwicks and 16 Royal Dublin Fusiliers of whom Privates Delany and McCarthy died on Christmas Eve.

5509 RIFLEMAN
R. BARNETT
THE RIFLE BRIGADE
19TH DECEMBER 1914 AGE 15

תנצבה

From top left clockwise:
• Ploegsteert Wood Military Cemetery
• Rifle House Cemetery
• Grave of under age 15 year old
Rifleman R. Barnett in Rifle House Cemetery

On leaving the cemetery, turn right and after 200 metres you will find the Khaki Chums' Cross (4E-1) which commemorates the Christmas Truce. About 200 metres behind the cross is the spot where Bruce Bairnsfather fraternised with the Saxons. Walk into St Yves- the first cottage on the right (4E-2) is where Bairnsfather drew some of his first cartoons, commemorated by a plaque put up by his biographers, Major Tonie and Mrs Valmai Holt.

Plaque to Bruce Bairnsfather *Annette George*

Having walked through the village along "St. Yves Avenue" (sometimes referred to as "London Avenue"), you will arrive at a T junction and the sunken road (4F-1) made famous by Captain Robert Hamilton. It was here, (see photo p. 75) hidden from German snipers, that he and his subalterns enjoyed a picnic on 2nd January 1915. The Royal Warwicks' front line was on the embankment facing you and the Germans' trenches were a mere 70 to 80 yards on the other side along the line of trees. Go left at the T junction and at the top of the sunken road you will come to a crossing of road and path (3F-2) where Lieutenant Drummond took a photograph of the Royal Warwicks and Saxons in No Man's Land (see p. 63). Take the path on the left which leads to the Khaki Chums Cross and retrace your steps along "Mud Lane" to "Mud Corner". Soon after, bear left on a path that will take you into the Wood.

Enter the Wood and after 250 metres Toronto Avenue Cemetery (5D-3), designed by G.H. Goldsmith, is down the path on your left. The 78 Australian casualties date from the Battle of Messines in 1917. Continue into the Wood and after 400 metres you will reach Ploegsteert Wood Military Cemetery (5D-1) on the right. It consists of a number of regimental plots including the original one started by the 1/Somerset Light Infantry. There are 28 of this Battalion's graves which date from December 1914; 26 were killed in the attack of 19th December including Captains Charles Maud, Robert Orr and Frank Bradshaw. Also buried here is the London Rifle Brigade's Private Arthur Bassingham who was killed on Christmas Eve. The cemetery was designed by W.H. Cowlishaw. Further on (6E-1) is the beautiful Rifle House Cemetery (if you are lucky there may be a host of butterflies to greet you), first used by the Rifle Brigade in November 1914. It was also designed by W.H. Cowlishaw. There are 230 burials including those of Captain the Hon. Richard Morgan-Grenville and Captain the Hon. Reginald Prittie.

Now return to "L' Auberge" and your car... after more refreshment, drive south for 500 metres to Strand Military Cemetery on the left (6A-4). It is situated at

LANCASHIRE COTTAGE CEMETERY 1914-1918

THIS CEMETERY WAS
DEDICATED BY THE
BISHOP OF LONDON
CHAPLAIN TO THE
REGIMENT ON EASTER
DAY 4TH APRIL 1915
IN GRATEFUL MEMORY OF THE FALLEN

From top left clockwise:
* *Lancashire Cottage Cemetery*
* *Plaque commemorating dedication of LRB Cemetery in 1915*
* *London Rifle Brigade Cemetery*

"Charing Cross" at the start of the "Strand" along which soldiers entered the Wood. It was started in October 1914. It contains 1,143 World War I graves (including one of five brothers killed in the War, Alfred Souls) and 82 World War II casualties of May 1940. It was designed by Charles Holden.

Further on south you will reach the village of Ploegsteert (8A). At the roundabout take the first exit and park on the left. You will see the Town Hall and to the left of the main door is the distinctive Churchill Plaque. Winston Churchill resigned as First Lord of the Admiralty following the fiasco at Gallipoli in 1915 and decided "to do his bit" at the Front as CO of the 6/ Royal Scots Fusiliers who manned trenches south east of the Wood in early 1916.

To the left of the Town Hall enter the Churchyard where there are nine British graves including that of Major George Hastings who was the acting CO of the 1/ Hants when he died on 19th December 1914, aged 44.

Now drive south for 500 metres and park on the right by London Rifle Brigade Cemetery, another designed by Charles Holden. It was begun by units of the 4th Division and named after the London Rifle Brigade which has 22 burials. Casualties in December 1914 include a Royal Dublin Fusilier, Private John Cashman, aged 19, who died on Christmas Day, two from the Rifle Brigade, Lieutenant Roger Ludovic Moore, aged 24, of the Somerset Light Infantry who died on 20th possibly from wounds sustained the previous day, one Royal Warwick and Private J.P. Finnigan of the East Lancs who died on Christmas Day.

The grave of Private Finnigan of the East Lancs who died on Christmas Day
Alan Reed

On Easter Day 1915, the cemetery was dedicated by the Bishop of London, Dr. A.F. Winnington-Ingram, the London Rifle Brigade's Honorary Chaplain. In June 1927 Lieutenant General Sir H.F.M. Wilson (late GOC 4th Division) unveiled a tablet to commemorate the dedication and to remember the 1,922 officers and other ranks of the Brigade who died in the War.

Drive back to the roundabout at Ploegsteert and turn right. After 1.2 kilometres stop on the right by Lancashire Cottage Cemetery (7D-3), another Holden design. It was started in November 1914 by the 1/ East Lancs (84 graves) and the 1/ Hants (56 graves). In all there are 269 burials including 13 Germans. One kilometre further on is the Calvary at the crossroads at Le Gheer (6F-2). Turn left and drive through the "Birdcage" (5F-3) and to the sunken road (4F-1) where you walked earlier on.

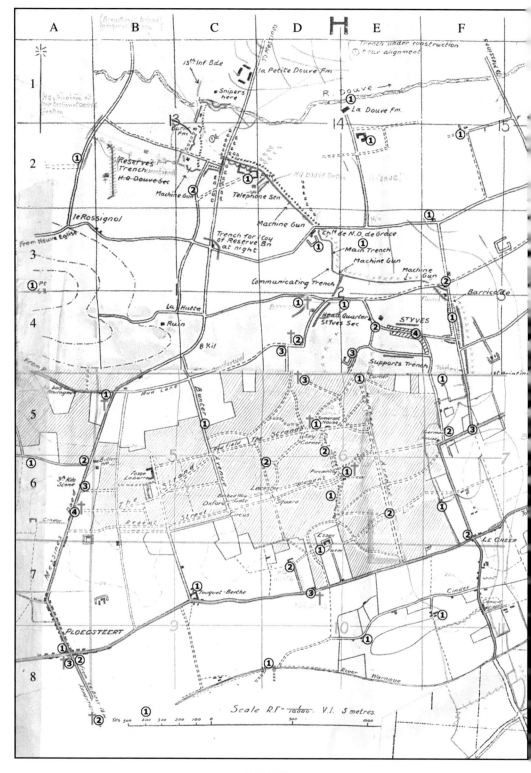

MAP VI
DETAILED MAP OF THE PLUGSTREET WOOD AREA
DECEMBER 1914

Map VI opposite is to be used in connection with Map IV.

GRID REFERENCES below are for paths, buildings, corners etc. in and around Plugstreet Wood using British and in some cases German names.

1E	1	La Douve Farm (in German: Wasserburg = Moated Castle)
2A	1	Irish Farm
2C	1	Seaforth Farm (in German: Englander Farm = Farm of the English)
	2	Fusilier Farm
2E	1	Avenue Farm (in German: Douve Farm)
2F	1	Grey Farm (in German: Abgebrannte Farm = Burnt Down Farm)
3A	1	Hill 63
3D	1	Anton's Farm (in German: Heide Schlösschen = Little Castle of the Heath)
3E	1	Site of Bruce Bairnsfather's truce
3F	1	Bayern Farm on Ash Avenue (in German: Bayern-Strasse = Bavaria Street)
	2	Broken Tree House(s) (in German: Söldner-Häuser = Mercenary's Houses) and site of Lieutenant Drummond's photo
4D	1	Prowse Point and Military Cemetery
	2	Mud Corner and Cemetery
	3	Poole's Cottage- named after the CO of 1/ Royal Warwicks
4E	1	Leval Cottage (in German: Yves Schloss = Chateau Yves) and Khaki Chums' Cross
	2	Bairnsfather's plaque at site where he drew his first cartoons
	3	Moated Farm on Rotten Row
	4	London Avenue or St. Yves Avenue
4F	1	Site of Captain Hamilton's truce and of picnic in sunken road on 2nd January
5B	1	Hyde Park Corner and Ploegsteert Memorial with Berks Cemetery Extension and Hyde Park Corner (Royal Berks) Cemetery
5C	1	Bunhill Row named after the HQ of the London Rifle Brigade in Finsbury (was Bunter Avenue until 27th December)
5D	1	Somerset House (HQ of 1/Somerset Light Infantry) and Ploegsteert Wood Military Cemetery
	2	Fleet Street
	3	Toronto Avenue Cemetery
5E	1	Dead Horse Corner
5F	1	Maximes and Hull's Burnt Farm named after Brigadier General Charles Hull of 10th Brigade
	2	German House
	3	Second House and area of "The Birdcage"

6A	1	The Piggeries
	2	Report Centre
	3	Charing Cross
	4	Strand Military Cemetery
6D	1	Haymarket
	2	Plugstreet Hall
6E	1	Rifle House (HQ of 1/ Rifle Brigade) and Cemetery
	2	Hampshire Lane
6F	1	Tourist Avenue
	2	Le Gheer Calvary
7C	1	Touquet-Berthe Farm
7D	1	Essex Farm- not to be confused with Essex Farm Cemetery and Advanced Dressing Station north of Ypres
	2	Hants Farm (HQ of 1/ Hampshires)
	3	Lancashire Cottage (HQ of 1/ East Lancs) and Cemetery
7F	1	Lancashire Support Farm
8A	1	Aux Trois Amis (estaminet)
	2	Au Lion d'Or (estaminet)
	3	Ploegsteert Churchyard
8B	1	London Support Farm
	2	London Rifle Brigade Cemetery
8D	1	McKenna Bridge named after the then Home Secretary
8E	1	Lawrence or Laurence Farm (HQ of 6/ Royal Scots Fusiliers with Winston Churchill as their CO in early 1916)

IV CHRISTMAS TRUCES AFTER 1914:

The authorities clamped down on further fraternisation- the threat of court martial was enough to discourage officers from sanctioning future "friendliness". It is generally believed that the only truces were in 1914, however, there is documentary evidence of other truces being held on a limited scale in not only 1915 but also 1916 and 1917.

In *Scots Guards on the Western Front 1915-1918*, Wilfrid Ewart writes about a truce that took place in 1915 at Aubers Ridge north of Loos in France: "For too brief- all too brief minutes there is peace and goodwill among the trenches." As in 1914 the Germans were the prime movers. The Germans (Bavarians of the 95th Bavarian Reserve Infantry Regiment) exchanged "cigars and pieces of sausages, and sauerkraut and concentrated coffee for cigarettes and bully beef and ration biscuits and tobacco." They held a conversation in broken English: "What sort of trenches have you?" The reply was heartfelt: "Rotten! Knee deep in mud and water. Not fit for pigs."

Further south at Monchy, east of Arras, Serjeant I.L. Read of the Leicestershire Regiment witnessed a meeting of Germans and Leicesters in No Man's Land: "The Germans offered their water-bottles which, we were told afterwards, contained Schnapps or coffee." After a few minutes a British officer blew his whistle to bring his men back to the trenches. Read includes in his book his sketch of the meeting

I.L. Read's drawing of the 8/ Leicesters' and Hanoverians' Christmas Truce in 1915

between the 8/ Leicesters and the 73rd Hanover Fusiliers. His comments about the experience are: "What a War! What would some of our armchair military experts at home advise now? In that moment the tremendous truth dawned on us: that men find it next to impossible to hate or fight when they are cold and wet. Someone echoed our feelings with 'what are we fighting for anyhow?' Truth to tell, just then we had forgotten."

Lieutenant Raymond Asquith, son of Herbert Asquith the Prime Minister, was angry that his father had used his influence to secure him a safe Intelligence job behind the lines and he was concerned at how "wretched and contemptible it would appear if he accepted it." He did so briefly during which time he was at least able to employ his legal skills on 18 January 1916 when he acted as a 'prisoner's friend' in defence of Captain Sir Iain Colquhoun of the 1/ Scots Guards for allowing his men to fraternise with Germans on Christmas Day 1915 near Laventie, after clear orders that a repetition of the armistices of 1914 was not to be repeated. The Court Martial decided that he should be "reprimanded" but Field Marshal Haig overturned the sentence due to Sir Iain's "distinguished conduct in the field". Asquith returned to front line action in May 1916. He died on 15th September during the Battle of the Somme.

In *This Foul Thing Called War*, a biography about Brigadier General R.J. Kentish, his nephew Basil writes that "The Germans tried this (the truce) again in subsequent years at various places. It was sternly forbidden by the powers that were, and, in 1916, two officers in the Brigade of Guards were court-martialled, one being acquitted."

There is evidence of at least one truce at Christmas in 1916. Private Ronald Mackinnon of Princess Patricia's Canadian Light Infantry described how at Vimy Ridge, German and Canadian soldiers shared Christmas greetings and exchanged presents: "Christmas Eve was pretty stiff, sentry- go up to the hip in mud of course… We had a truce on Christmas Day and our German friends were quite friendly. They came over to see us and we traded bully beef for cigars."

According to Private John Hall of 4/ Worcestershire Regiment at Christmas in 1917, "parties of German and British officers met on no-man's-land and were having cordial conversations with an exchange of souvenirs." He was in trenches near Ypres and watched the scene unfold from the parapet: "Several parties met like this for several hours."

ACKNOWLEDGEMENTS

We should like to express our special thanks to the following:

- Tom Morgan for offering comments that were unfailingly apposite and for providing information and leads for a plethora of our questions (www.hellfirecorner.co.uk)

- Ruth Smith for her excellent design and artwork (www.damsoncreative.co.uk)

Below we have combined Acknowledgements and Bibliography/Sources. We have tried to acknowledge those who have assisted and advised us and the authors and publications which we have referred to. We have been struck by the generosity of authors and owners of photographs and documents who have been most helpful in allowing us to use their material. We have attempted to trace all copyright holders with the occasional lack of success. If we have overlooked anyone, we offer our sincerest apologies and promise to include your name in the next edition.

- Baker, Chris… for his excellent website *Long, Long, Trail* www.1914-1918.net/

- Bell, David, Imperial War Museum... for his help with the museum's photographs

- Bennett, Stephanie, Curator, Royal Regiment of Fusiliers Museum (Royal Warwickshire)… use of photographs

- Bott, Liz… Translation of Leutnant Johannes Niemann's diary account of football match at Frelinghien

- Butler, Dominic, Assistant Curator, Lancashire Infantry Museum… use of extracts from diary of Edward Roe

- Cave, David… permission to use Lieutenant Guy Cave's correspondence

- Cleaver, Alan… use of material on the website www.christmastruce.co.uk

- Dendooven, Dominiek… use of photographs from the In Flanders Fields Museum

- Holt, Tonie and Valmai… for kindly agreeing to write a foreword to the book

- Kerr, James… for photographs taken on various trips to the Western front sites

- Matthews, Beverley, Archivist Tonbridge School… information about Lieutenant Guy Cave

- Morgan, Harry… allowing us to quote from his father's memoirs *Harry's War* Rydan Press 2002

- Sayell, George… work on maps

- Towndrow, Francis… information about Private William Setchfield (RWR)

- Verhaeghe, Claude… information about Plugstreet Wood

- Warby, Mark… for his great efforts in providing us with Bruce Bairnsfather material and permission for its use

ARCHIVES, LIBRARIES and MUSEUMS:

- British Newspaper Museum, Colindale
- Commonwealth War Graves Commission- www.cwgc.org
- Highlanders' Museum, Inverness
- Imperial War Museum
- In Flanders Fields Museum, Ypres
- Lancashire Infantry Museum, Preston
- National Archives
- Royal Hampshire Regimental Museum, Winchester
- Royal Irish Fusiliers Museum, Armagh
- Royal Regiment of Fusiliers Museum (Royal Warwickshire), Warwick
- South West Heritage Trust, Taunton

OFFICIAL SOURCES:

National Archives:

- III Corps WO95/ 668 and 669
- 4th Division   WO95/ 1440 and 1441
- 10th Infantry Brigade   W095/ 1477 and 1478
- 11th Infantry Brigade   WO95/ 1488
- 32nd Brigade Royal Field Artillery   WO95/ 1467
- 10th Field Ambulance   WO95/ 1474
- 1/ East Lancashire WO95/ 1498
- 1/ Hampshire   WO95/ 1495
- 31st Heavy Battery RGA   WO95/ 230
- 1/5 London Regiment (London Rifle Brigade)   WO95/ 1498
- 1/ Rifle Brigade   W095/ 1496
- 2/ Royal Dublin Fusiliers   WO95/ 1481
- 1/ Royal Irish Fusiliers   WO95/ 1482
- 1/ Royal Warwicks   WO95/ 1484

- 2/ Seaforth Highlanders   WO95/ 1483 and WO95/ 1440

INDIVIDUALS' SOURCES:

- Bairnsfather, Lieutenant Bruce   Machine-Gun Corps officer 1/ Royal Warwicks Cartoons ©2014 Estate of Barbara Bruce Littlejohn

- Barnett, Private A.   1/ Royal Warwicks   *Warwick and Warwickshire Advertiser* 30th January 1915

- Barrs, Serjeant H.A.   Cyclist Corps   *Warwick and Warwickshire Advertiser* 9th January 1915   www.christmastruce.co.uk

- Bates, Major (later Colonel) Arthur   London Rifle Brigade   *Short History of the London Rifle Brigade*

- Beck, Regimental Serjeant Major   1/ Royal Warwicks   Diary   Dorchester Records Office

- Beckett, Captain J.D.M.   1/ Hampshire   National Archives   WO95/ 1488 *Report to 11th Infantry Brigade "on proceedings to the front of Hampshire Regiment trench on Christmas Day"*

- Black, Lieutenant Frank   1/ Royal Warwicks   Letters   IWM 82/3/1

- Calder, Corporal J.S.   London Rifle Brigade   Letter   *The Essex Chronicle*   15th January1915

- Cave, Lieutenant Guy   1/ Royal Warwicks   Letter   December 31st   by kind permission of David Cave

- Chappell, Rifleman Jack   London Rifle Brigade   National Archives   WO95/ 1498

- Cook, Corporal Arthur   1/ Somerset Light Infantry   Diary   Somerset Record Office

- Cooke, Private Walter   1/ Royal Warwicks   Letter   *Rugby Advertiser*   January 16th 1915   www.christmastruce.co.uk

- Coulson, Lance Corporal   London Rifle Brigade   *Hertfordshire Mercury*   16th January 1915

- Day, Private Alfred   Royal Warwicks   Letter   *Warwick and Warwickshire Advertiser*   January 16th 1915   www.christmastruce.co.uk

- Dixon, Private H.   1/ Royal Warwicks   Letter   www.christmastruce.co.uk

- Donaldson, Captain Geoffrey   1/7 Royal Warwicks   Diaries and Letters   IWM 69/ 25/ 1

- Drummond, Lieutenant Cyril   135th Battery Royal Field Artillery attached 10th Brigade   Transcript of Memories of the Great War   IWM   87/56/1

- Ewart, Wilfrid   *Scots Guards on the Western Front 1915-1918*   Rich and Cowan Ltd. 1934

- Fairs, Private E.W.   London Rifle Brigade   Letter   *Croydon Advertiser and Surrey County Recorder*   9th January 1915

- Ferguson, Corporal John   2/ Seaforth Highlanders   from article *The Truce of 1914*   by Thomas Vinciguerra in *The New York Times*   2005

- Furneaux, Private   Rifle Brigade   Letter   *Western Mail*   1915

- Gaunt, Lieutenant   1/ Royal Warwicks   Diary   IWM   75/78/1

- Grigg, Rifleman Selby   London Rifle Brigade   IWM   84/9/1

- Hall, John   4/ Worcesters   from   *The Great War Magazine*   *Issue 14*   *July 2004*   Article by Brian V. Thomas   *The Christmas Truce of 1917*

- Hamilton, Captain Robert   1/ Royal Warwicks   Diary   Andrew Hamilton

- Hawksley, Major   RFA   *Daily Telegraph*   30th May 2013

- Hull, Brigadier General Charles   4th Division Report from 10th Infantry Brigade   January 1915

- Hunter-Weston, General Aylmer   National Archives WO95/ 1488 11th Brigade

- Hutchings, Private Bertie Cecil   1/ Hampshire   Letter   Royal Hampshire Museum

- Judd, Corporal Samuel   Diary   IWM

- Latham, Bryan   London Rifle Brigade   IWM   82/ 1925

- Layton, Private G.   1/ Royal Warwicks   Letter   *Birmingham Weekly Post*   January 16th 1915   www.christmastruce.co.uk

- Lintott, Private Richard   London Rifle Brigade   IWM   86/66/1   www.christmastruce.co.uk

- Lloyd-Burch, David   10th Field Ambulance attached 4th Division   National Archives   WO95/ 1474 (10th Field Ambulance)   IWM   87/26/1

- Mackay, Private John   2/ Seaforth Highlanders   *Letter in Ayr Advertiser 28th* January 1915

- Mattey, Private   1/ Royal Warwicks

- Munro, Private Colin   2/ Seaforth Highlanders   Letter   *Ayr Advertiser*   14 January 1915

- Packe, Private Edward   1/ Somerset Light Infantry   from *Good Old Somersets-An 'Old Contemptible' Battalion in 1914*   Brian Gillard   Matador   2004

- Pentelow, Private W.   Letter   *Northamptonshire Daily Echo*   1915

- Percy, Private W.R.M.   IWM   82/ 1925 and K12/ 460 (Pamphlet entitled *Peace and Goodwill*   National Peace Council)

- Philpotts, Serjeant J.   Interview BBC Great War Series correspondence   IWM 75/ 78/ 1

- Pratt, Private Charlie 1/ Royal Warwicks   Letter   *Evesham Journal* January 16th 1915

- Pulteney, Lieutenant General Sir William CO III Corps   from *Meetings in No Man's Land* Constable and Robinson   2007

- Read, Serjeant I.L.   *Of Those We Loved* Pentland Press   1994

- Reading, Rifleman   1/ Rifle Brigade   Letter   *Buckinghamshire Examiner* Friday 8th January 1915

- Roe, Private Edward 1/ East Lancashire   *Diary of an Old Contemptible From Mons to 1914-1919* edited by Peter Downham   Pen and Sword   2004

- Setchfield, Private William   1/ Royal Warwicks   Letter   *Newark Advertiser* Jan 6 1915

- Smith, Private Alfred   1/ Royal Warwicks   *Midlands Daily Telegraph* Tuesday 5th January   *Warwick and Warwickshire Advertiser* 16th January www.christmastruce.co.uk

- Smith-Dorrien, General Sir Horace   *Memories of Forty Eight Years' Service* John Murray   1925

- Unwin, Captain Lancelot 1/ Hampshire   Message re. end of Truce   Royal Hampshire Regiment Museum

- Williams, Rifleman H.G.R.   London Rifle Brigade   Letter to IWM

- Zehmisch, Leutnant Kurt   134th Saxon Regiment   Diary   In Flanders Fields Museum, Ieper   Translation by Bruce White

PUBLISHED SOURCES:

- *Antelope, The*   The Royal Regiment of Fusiliers Museum (Royal Warwickshire), Warwick

- Bairnsfather, Bruce   *Bullets and Billets* Grant Richards   1916

- Bairnsfather, Bruce   *Fragments from France* The Bystander   1916

- Bairnsfather, Bruce   *From Mud to Mufti* Grant Richards   1919

- Bairnsfather, Bruce   *One Night in Flanders* The American Magazine December 1929

- Brown, Malcolm   *The Christmas Truce 1914: The British Story in Meetings in No Man's Land* Constable and Robinson   2007

- Brown, Malcolm and Seaton, Shirley   *The Christmas Truce* Papermac   1994

- Chasseaud, Peter *Topography of Armageddon* Mapbooks 1991

- Coleman, Frederic *From Mons to Ypres with French* William Briggs 1916

- Dendooven, Dominiek *Kurt Zehmisch and the Great War in Waasten* In Flanders Fields Magazine July 2000

- Edmonds, Brigadier-General Sir James *History of the Great War based on official documents by direction of the Historical Section of the Committee of Imperial Defence. Military Operations. France and Belgium, 1915: [Vol.1] Winter 1914-15* compiled by Brigadier-General Sir James E. Edmonds and Captain G.C. Wynne (London: Macmillan, 1927)

- Ferro, Marc, Brown, Malcolm, Cazals, Rémy, Mueller, Olaf *Meetings in No Man's Land* Constable and Robinson Ltd. 2007

- Gillard, Brian Good Old Somersets- *An 'Old Contemptible' Battalion in 1914* Matador 2004

- Haig, Field Marshal Sir Douglas *War Diaries and Letters* 1914-1918 edited by Gary Sheffield and John Browne Weidenfeld and Nicolson 2005

- Hamilton, Andrew and Reed, Alan *Meet at Dawn, Unarmed* Dene House Publishing 2009

- Hamilton, Andrew and Reed, Alan *Stolen Lives* Dene House Publishing 2014

- Kentish, Basil *This Foul Thing Called War* The Book Guild 1997

- Kingsford, C.L. *The Story of the Royal Warwickshire Regiment* Newnes 1921

- Lawrence, Lieutenant Colonel G.H. 1/ East Lancashire included in *Diary of an Old Contemptible from Mons to Baghdad 1914-1919* edited by Peter Downham Pen and Sword 2004

- Maurice, Sir Frederick, Brigadier-General: *The History of London Rifle Brigade* Constable and Co 1921

- Morgan, Harry 1/ Royal Warwicks *Harry's War* Rydan 2002

- Roe, Private Edward 1/ East Lancashire *Diary of an Old Contemptible From Mons to Baghdad 1914-1919* edited by Peter Downham Pen and Sword 2004

- Scott, Peter T *Christmas Day in Plugstreet* *Stand-To Magazine* Winter 1984

- Spagnoly, Tony and Smith, Ted *A Walk Round Plugstreet* Leo Cooper 2003

- Spagnoly, Tony and Smith, Ted *Salient Points 5* Leo Cooper

- Thomas, Brian V. in *The Great War Magazine, Issue 14* *The Christmas Truce of 1917* July 2004

- **114** Weber, Thomas *Hitler's First War* Oxford University Press 2010

- Weber, Dr. Thomas in *New Evidence of First World War Christmas Truces Uncovered*   University of Aberdeen News   15th December 2010

- Weintraub, Stanley *Silent Night*   Pocket Books   2002

- Westlake, Ray *British Battalions in France and Belgium 1914*   Leo Cooper 1997

- Williamson, Anne   *A Patriot's Progress - Henry Williamson and the First World War*   Sutton   1998

- Wilson, Sergeant Hugh   *Angels and Heroes- The Story of a Machine Gunner with the Royal Irish Fusiliers August 1914 to April 1915*   compiled by Amanda Moreno and David Truesdale for the Royal Irish Fusiliers Museum   2004

- Woollcott, Alexander   By *Word of Mouth*   *The American Legion Magazine* July 1931

- Wray, Frank and Maurice   *Christmas 1914*   The Army Quarterly Vol. XCVII October 1968

WEBSITES:

- Chris Baker's *Long, Long, Trail* www.1914-1918.net/ (website nominated for an award from the Chartered Institute of Librarians and Information Professionals)

- Tom Morgan's *Hellfire Corner* www.fylde.demon.co.uk

- Christmas Truce 1914   *Operation Plum Puddings* www.christmastruce.co.uk

- Commonwealth War Graves Commission   www.cwgc.org

INDEX

There are main headings for:

- **Battles and Offensives**
- **British Expeditionary Force**
- **Cemeteries and Memorials**
- **Newspapers, Periodicals**
- **Places in Belgium, France, U.K. and elsewhere**
- **Soldiers mentioned in the text**

A

Aisne, river 12, 89, 93
"Alfs", "Berts" "Bills" 27, 42, 74, 93, 94
Angel of Mons 87
Asquith, H.H., Prime Minister 46, 108
Asquith, Lieutenant Raymond 86, 108

B

Battles and Offensives:
  Gallipoli 103
  Messines 99, 101
  Méteren 89
  Mons 87
  Passchendaele 25, 85
  Selle, River 95
  Somme 13, 66, 69, 92, 95, 99, 108
  1st Ypres 12
  2nd Ypres 73, 90, 94

Bairnsfather cartoons/ sketches 4, 13, 17, 34, 35, 42, 44, 45, 49, 60, 61, 74, 80, 93, 95, 101
Barbed wire entanglements 24, 31, 32, 33, 36, 37, 60, 61, 64, 65, 66, 83
Batman Officer's servant 35, 36, 47, 58, 89
Bavarians 53, 107
BBC Great War Series 59
Beefeater 92
Black Hat Gang 44, 90, 91
Boer War 11, 59, 88
Breastworks 22, 38, 40, 58

British Expeditionary Force 11, 12, 14, 16, 20, 93

Army:
  First 47
  Second 47, 64

Brigades:
  10th 11,12,17,19, 21, 24, 30, 32, 34, 47, 64, 67, 75, 77, 78, 81, 83, 84,
  11th 11, 12, 17, 19, 20, 21, 27, 30, 31, 34, 38, 43, 47, 52, 64, 65, 68, 69, 70, 71, 72, 73, 77, 78, 79
  12th 19, 30
  18th 12

Corps:
  II 29, 36
  III 19, 36, 80

Divisions:
  4th 19, 27, 32, 33, 34, 57, 65, 70, 72, 81, 83, 103
  5th 82

Regiments/ Battalions:
  Brigade of Guards 108
  1st Cavalry Division 21
  Cheshire 93
  1/5 (City of London) London (London Rifle Brigade) 11, 20, 21, 22, 26, 31, 38, 40, 41, 43, 46, 49, 53, 54, 55, 57, 58, 59, 60, 62, 67, 68, 73, 76, 80, 84, 96
  1/ East Lancashire 20, 22, 27, 35, 40, 43, 44, 48, 56, 61, 64, 68, 72, 73, 84, 86, 96, 103
  3/ Grenadier Guards 86
  1/ Hampshire 20, 21, 22, 24, 27, 30, 31, 36, 38, 43, 44, 48, 53, 60, 64, 67, 68, 71, 72, 73, 83, 84, 96, 103

2/ Inniskillings 69
8/ Leicesters 107
Norfolk 59
Princess Patricia's Light Infantry 108
1/ Rifle Brigade 20, 21, 30, 31, 32, 36, 38, 47, 48, 49, 51, 52, 58, 67, 69, 70, 71, 72, 82, 84, 96, 97, 101, 103
Royal Army Medical Corps (RAMC) 56
2/ Royal Dublin Fusiliers 19, 21, 26, 29, 30, 35, 78, 80, 83, 96, 103
Royal Engineers (9th Field Company) 24, 66, 77, 80, 97
Royal Field Artillery 11, 32, 51, 52, 54, 63, 70, 81
6/ Royal Fusiliers 90
1/ Royal Irish Fusiliers 19, 21, 26, 27, 30, 34, 44, 55, 69, 71, 82, 83, 85, 96, 99
1/ Royal Warwicks 11, 12, 13, 17, 19, 21, 24, 25, 26, 27, 30, 32, 34, 35, 36, 37, 41, 42, 43, 44, 46, 47, 48, 49, 51, 52, 54, 55, 57-60, 62-68, 70, 71, 72, 74, 75, 77, 81, 82, 83, 88-90, 93-95, 96, 99, 101,103
1/ 7 Royal Warwicks 86
1/ Scots Guards 107, 108
2/ Seaforth Highlanders 19, 21, 27, 34, 37, 42, 44, 48, 51, 55, 70, 71, 74, 75, 81, 83, 96
Signallers 71
1/ Somerset Light Infantry 20, 21, 22, 24, 25, 30, 31, 32, 38, 40, 41, 43, 47, 49, 51, 58, 61, 65, 66, 67, 68, 70, 71-74, 76, 78, 81, 84, 85, 91-92, 96, 97, 101
3rd Warwickshire Militia 93
4/ Worcesters 108

Bully beef 48, 49, 75, 107, 108
Burials 11, 67-69, 73, 83, 84

C

Cameras 62, 63
Carols 11, 36, 37, 41, 42
Cavalry 12

Cemeteries and Memorials:

Berks Cemetery Extension 99
Hyde Park Corner (Royal Berks) 99

La Ferté-sous-Jouarre Memorial 93
Lancashire Cottage 96, 103
London Rifle Brigade 40, 96, 103
Menin Gate, Ypres 73, 90
Mud Corner 99
Ploegsteert Churchyard 31, 96, 103
Ploegsteert Memorial 69, 96, 99
Ploegsteert Wood Military 40, 67, 97, 101
Prowse Point 34, 96
Rifle House 31, 69, 74, 96, 101
Strand Military 97, 101
Toronto Avenue 101

Censorship 85, 86
Champagne 27, 30, 90
Chaplain 12, 103
Chasseaud, Dr. Peter 29
Chef 59
Christmas Food 58-59
Christmas Trees 11, 36, 37, 42
Christmas Truces, other 107-108
Churchill, Winston 103
Cigars, cigarettes, tobacco 29, 36, 37, 44, 46, 48, 49, 56, 59, 70, 107, 108
Collection of bodies 67-70
Commonwealth (Imperial) War Graves Commission 40, 69
Concertinas and cornets 35
Conscientious Objectors 89
Corduroy roads 24, 25
Corelli, Marie 94
Court Martial 85, 108

D

Doudney, Rev. Charles 12
Douve, river 17, 26
Doyle, Sir Arthur Conan 13
Dugout 24, 26, 44, 48, 91
Dunalley, Lord 69

E

Estaminets 27, 93, 95
Exchanges in No Man's Land 48-49

F

Fatigues 66, 67
Fleas 26, 85

Football 54-57
Forestier Walker, G. 29
Fortnum and Mason 26, 35
Fritz 49, 51, 85

G

Gas attacks 90
George V, King 26, 46
German Army:

XIX Corps 17, 20, 52, 83

16th Bavarian Infantry Reserve 82
95th Bavarian Infantry Reserve 107
73rd Hanover Fusiliers 107
6th Jäger 20, 62
132nd Saxon 52
133rd Saxon 52, 56
134th Saxon 12, 17, 20, 26, 33, 41, 44,
    52, 54, 63, 67, 82, 83

Germans 11, 12, 13, 29, 30, 31, 32, 34,
    35, 36, 42, 44, 46, 49, 51, 52-53, 54, 55,
    56, 59, 60, 61, 62
German bands 41
Glenalmond, Trinity College, Perthshire 88
Goatskin waistcoats 34
Goldsmith, George IWGC Architect 93,
    99, 101

H

"Hell" 12, 13,
Hereford Detention Barracks 89, 94
Humour 26, 45, 53

I

Information/ intelligence gathering 64-66

J

Jack Johnson coalboxes 78
John Hassall School of Art 93, 94
Judge, Jack "Tipperary" 41

K

Khaki Chums' Cross 56, 99

L

Landsturmers 53
Landwehr 53

Lice 85
Loopholes 64, 77

M

"Making Good" 66-67
Mail 70
Marne, river 12, 89
Maurice, Major General historian LRB 55,
    67
Meet at Dawn, Unarmed by Hamilton/
    Reed 7, 8, 9, 12, 89, 90
Mud 14, 20, 24, 25, 26, 31, 34, 40, 57,
    80, 85, 108
Music 37, 41-42, 74

N

Newspapers, Periodicals:

Ayr Advertiser 42
Birmingham Post 47
Bystander 74
Carlisle Journal 86
Tatler 44, 91
Times 36, 56
Warwick and Warwickshire Advertiser 12

O

"Over by Christmas" 12
"Old Bill" 25, 74, 93, 94
"Old Contemptible" 92
Orpen, Sir William artist 78

P

Parapet 27, 35, 44, 108
Photographs 11, 48, 70
Pickelhaube German helmet 37, 68

Places:

Belgium:
Aerschot 61
Comines-Warneton 54
Dinant 61
Hill 63 17
Le Gheer 17, 20, 27, 73, 103
Louvain 61
Messines (Mesen) 1, 7, 19, 54, 82
Nieuwpoort 17
Ploegsteert 17, 20, 21, 61, 103

St. Yves (St. Yvon) 17, 19, 20, 30, 35, 40, 44, 54, 55, 57, 59, 63, 73, 99, 101
Ypres Salient 17, 108

France:
Armentières 12, 17, 19, 90, 94
Arras 107
Aubers Ridge 107
Frelinghien 30, 56
La Crèche 34, 35, 74, 83
La Ferté-sous-Jouarre 93
Laventie 108
Loos 107
Monchy 107
Nieppe 21, 83
Steenwerck 90
St. Omer 47
Verdun 17
Vimy Ridge 108

Germany:
Chemnitz 52

Plugstreet Wood Area:
Avenue 37
Bayern Farmhouse 63
Birdcage 31, 103
Bunhill Row 20-21
German House 31
Hunter Avenue 20-21, 66
Leicester Square 29
Mud (Muddy) Lane 24, 35, 99, 101
Piccadilly Circus 29
Plugstreet Hall 19
Somerset House 67
Strand 29
St. Yves Avenue 75
Sunken Road 63, 74, 75, 90, 101, 103
Touquet Berthe 22
Wasserburg 38

United Kingdom:
Ayr 44
Birmingham 54, 59
Bishopton, Warwicks 93
Eastbourne 59
Edinburgh 87
Evesham 43
Glasgow 60
Hamilton, Lanarkshire 88
Hereford 89
London 59, 61, 94
Newark, Notts 27

Oldbury 41
Stratford-on-Avon 88, 94
Taunton 91
Temple Balsall, Warwicks 41
Tunbridge Wells 91
Walton, Warwicks 88
Wroughton near Swindon 91

Poulton Palmer, Ronnie England rugby captain 99
Pope Benedict XV 13, 87
Prince of Wales 26
Princess Mary's Christmas Box 46, 74, 84
Prussians 52, 53, 67, 76
Pumps 20, 24, 76

R

Rations 27, 49, 107
Ration parties 27
Red Cross 67, 69
Rum 26, 42
Russia/ Russians 45, 52, 53, 86, 87

S

Sandhurst, Royal Military College 93
Saxons 21, 30, 37, 38, 44, 46, 47, 48, 51-54, 56, 57, 60, 67, 68, 70, 74, 75, 76, 99
Shells, shell fire 27, 30, 32, 40, 46, 58, 70, 74, 75, 90
Shell shock 91, 94
Snipers, sniper fire 27, 30, 58, 66, 70, 73, 75, 76, 77, 85

Soldiers, British:

Generals:
French, Field Marshal Sir John 20, 27, 40, 47, 76, 77, 78
Haig, General Sir Douglas 47
Hull, Brigadier General Charles 19, 47, 77, 78, 89
Hunter-Weston, Brigadier General Aylmer 20, 47, 77, 78
Pulteney, Lieutenant General Sir William 77, 78, 80, 93
Smith-Dorrien, General Sir Horace 29, 36, 47, 57, 64, 76, 77, 78, 80
Wilson, Major General Henry 19, 57, 77, 78, 103

Andrew, Rifleman LRB 62

Bairnsfather, Lieutenant Bruce RWR 25, 31, 36, 41, 49, 50, 55, 60, 70, 74, 78, 81, 82, 87, 90, 93-95, 99

Barnett, Private A. RWR 21, 25, 49, 82

Barrs, Serjeant Cyclist Corps 34

Bassingham, Rifleman Arthur LRB 40, 43, 96, 101

Bates, Major RB 31, 43

Beck, RSM George RWR 48, 54, 68

Beckett, Captain J.D.M. HR 53, 64, 68

Black, Lieutenant Frank RWR 46, 52, 78

Boyd, Private Robert 2/ Inniskillings 69

Bradshaw, Captain Frank SLI 31, 99, 101

Calder, Lance Corporal LRB 38, 41, 53, 81

Carter, Private RWR 26

Cashman, Private John RDF 96, 103

Cave, Lieutenant Guy RWR 13, 25, 26, 42, 48, 62, 66, 68, 78, 81, 89-91

Chappell, Rifleman Jack LRB 59, 67

Coleman, Frederic 1st Cavalry Division 21, 25, 43, 47, 49, 64, 67, 76

Colquhoun, Captain Sir Ian 1/ Scots Guards 108

Compton, Major SLI 47

Cook, Corporal Arthur SLI 22, 25, 26, 30, 32, 51, 61, 81, 85, 91-93

Cooke, Private Walter RWR 25, 41, 54, 58

Coulson, Lance Corporal LRB 22, 38, 40, 49, 54, 68, 81

Davie Private Jim SH 27, 37, 44, 70

Day, Private Alfred RWR 12, 48, 52, 59, 77

Delaney, Private T. RDF 34, 99

Dennys, Lieutenant K.G.G. SLI 84

Dixon, Private RWR 41

Donaldson, Captain Geoffrey 1/7 RWR 86, 95

Drummond, Lieutenant Cyril RFA 51, 52, 63, 70, 101

Fairs, Private RB 42, 46, 58, 81

Ferguson, Private John SH 51

Finnigan, Private J.P. ELR 40, 96, 103

Furneaux, Private Ernest RB 49, 58

Gaunt, Lieutenant K.M. RWR 24

Gregory, Private RWR 35, 36

Grigg, Rifleman LRB 62, 68

Hall, Private John 4/ Worcesters 108

Hamilton, Captain Robert RWR 12, 21, 26, 34-36, 44, 46, 48, 51, 52, 54, 55, 59, 70, 71, 74, 77, 78, 80, 81, 87-91, 93, 101

Henson, Lieutenant HR 67

Hawksley, Major RFA 54, 70, 81

Hill, Captain G.V.W. RIF 69

Hutchings, Private HR 38, 48, 60, 71

Jackson, Peter 57

Judd, Corporal Samuel RWR 82

Kentish, Brigadier R.J. 21, 26, 108

Latham, Private Bryan LRB 21, 80

Lawrence, Lieutenant Colonel G.H. ELR 56, 64

Layton, Private RWR 41, 51, 52, 68, 77

Le Mare, Lieutenant RIF 26

Lewis, Harold RFA 86, 87

Lintott, Rifleman Richard LRB 58

Lloyd-Burch, David 10th Field Ambulance 46, 67, 81

Mackay, Private John SH 42, 81

Mackinnon, Ronald Princess Patricia's Canadian LI 108

Mattey, Private RWR 60

Maud, Captain Charles SLI 31, 32, 67, 84, 101

McCarthy, Private Patrick RDF 34, 99

Montgomery, Lieutenant Bernard Law RWR 89

Moore, Lieutenant Roger SLI 103

Morgan, Private Harry RWR 44, 46, 48, 51, 60, 72

Morgan-Grenville, Captain the Hon. Richard George RB 31, 101

Munro, Private Colin SH 44, 48, 81

Orr, Captain Robert SLI 31, 67, 84, 101

Packe, Private Edward SLI 47, 49, 58, 65

Parker, Major George HR 31, 96

Pentelow, Private RB 42, 48, 53

Percy, Private W.R.M. LRB 53, 55, 62

Philpotts, Serjeant J. RWR 36, 42, 45, 59, 67, 82

Poole, Major A.J. RWR 47, 91

Pratt, Private Charlie RWR 42, 43

Prittie, the Hon. Reginald RB 31, 69, 101

Prophet, Colonel 10th Field Ambulance 46

Prowse, Major Charles SLI 99

Rea, Serjeant RWR 36

Read, I.L. 8/ Leicesters 107

Reading, Rifleman RB 49, 51, 82

Reagan, Private Jack RWR 60
Richards, Lieutenant C.E.M. ELR 56
Roe, Private Edward ELR 22, 27, 31, 35, 40, 45, 48, 61, 68, 72, 86
Setchfield, Private William RWR 27, 55, 62, 82
Simons, Rifleman N.H. RB 74
Smith, Private Alfred RWR 55, 58, 81
Somers-Smith, Captain LRB 60
Sperry, Private RWR 89
Sutton, Lieutenant Colonel SLI 32
Tapp, Private William RWR 12, 26, 30, 36, 47, 48, 49, 52, 54, 58, 66, 75, 77, 81
Tillyer, Lieutenant Richard RWR 47, 66
Turner, Rifleman LRB 62
Unwin, Captain HR 38, 72, 73
Wasey, Lieutenant Cyril RWR 44
Williams, Rifleman H.G.R. LRB 41, 60
Williamson, Lieutenant Henry LRB 26, 31, 46, 53, 68, 81
Wilson, Serjeant Hugh RIF 21, 27, 30, 55, 71, 72, 82
Wray brothers LRB 38, 49
Wrentmore, Frank SLI 31

Soldiers, German:

Hitler, Gefreiter Adolf 16th Bavarian Reserve Infantry 82
Holland, NCO 134th Saxon Reg 62
Huss, Private 134th Saxon Reg 37
Möckel, Private134th Saxon Reg 37
Niemann, Leutnant Johannes 133rd Saxon Reg 56
Zehmisch, Leutnant Kurt 134th Saxon Reg 33, 37, 38, 39, 44, 51, 54, 57, 62, 69, 75, 82

Souls, Private Alfred one of 5 brothers killed 103
Star shells 11, 31, 42
Stockings 27
Streets, William poet and miner 69
Strange happenings and coincidences 59-61
Stretcher-bearers 31, 40, 67

T

Territorials 11, 20, 21, 26, 86
"Tommy" 25, 26, 27, 32, 47, 56, 61-63, 81, 85, 91, 93
Tonbridge School 89
"Top Brass" 61, 77, 85
Trench foot 77
Trocadero Restaurant, Mayfair 59

U

Uhlan 67

W

Waiters Germans in England 29, 53
Ware, Sir Fabian Imperial War Graves Commission 69
Warnave, river 17
Wilhelm, Kaiser 12, 51
Williams, Harry "Tipperary" 41
Winnington-Ingram, Bishop of London 46, 103
Wounds, self-inflicted 27

Z

Zehmisch, Rudolph 33

The sunken lane at St. Yves- the trenches of 1/ Royal Warwicks were on the embankment to the right
J Kerr

The Christmas Truce meetings took place in No Man's Land between the German trenches in front of the trees and the Royal Warwicks' trenches on the embankment
J Kerr

RICHARDSON G. 8048
RICHARDSON G.2097b
RIDLEY T.
RIDLEY W. A.
RILEY A.
ROACH W.
ROBERTSON G. L.
ROBERTSON R.
ROBERTSON W.
ROBERTSON W. J.
ROBERTSON W. N.
ROBEY T.
ROBINSON G.
ROBINSON H.
ROBINSON J.
ROBINSON P.
ROBINSON R.
ROBSON A.
ROBSON E. H.
ROBSON J. 1652
ROBSON J. 1983
ROBSON R. 2359
ROBSON R. 7659
75 ROBSON T.
308 ROBSON T. R.
ROBSON T. W.
ROBSON W. C.
ROGERSON J.
ROOKE F. W.
ROSE S.
ROWBOTHAM J.
ROWDEN F. R.
ROYCE T.
RUDD J.
RYDER J. W.
SANDERSON E.
SANDERSON J. 2269
SANDERSON J. 20980
SANDERSON T. W.
SCALES D.
SCOTT A. J.
SCOTT F. J.
SCOTT J.
SCOTT R. 1883
SCOTT R. 8694
SCOTT W. T.
SCRIMSHAW J.
SCRIVENER J.E.
SCULLEY W.
SCURR S.
SEED H.
SEMOUR A.
SEVERN E.
SHAFTOE J.
SHANE E. E.
SHARKEY A.
SHARPE A.
SHAW J.E.
SHENTON J.
SHEPHERD J.
SHIELDS A.
SHINN A.
SHORTT J.
SIDDAL G. W.
SIDDLE W.
SIMMONDS M.
SIMPSON J.
SIMPSON T.
SIMPSON W.
SKELTON R.
SKIDMORE G.
SLACK B.
SLEE J. J.
SMAILES C.
SMAILES W. W.
SMALL H.
SMITH D.
SMITH E.
SMITH E. C.
SMITH E. L.
SMITH H.
SMITH H. F.
SMITH J. 1079
SMITH J. 1185
SMITH J. 4030
SMITH J. 8597

WAITE F. C.
WAKE T. H.
WAKE W. H.
WALKER A.
WALKER E. R.
WALKER J. W.
WALLACE W.
WALLER H.
WALTERS J.
WARD M. M.
WARD P.
WATERHOUSE C.
WATSON F.

ROYAL WARWICKSHIRE REGIMENT

LIEUT. COLONEL
LORING W. L.

MAJOR
LANCASTER J. C.

CAPTAIN
BRISCOE E. V.
CARLISLE-CROWE W. M.
McCORMICK J. H. G.
METHUEN C. O'B. H.
SCHOOLING E. C.
WALKER H. J. I.

LIEUTENANT
DEANE D.
FETHERSTONHAUGH-FRAMPTON P. T.
HUNTER N. F.
JOWITT A.
MACLAGAN G. S.
NICOLAI R. C.
TILLYER R.B.B.
WINDELER C. F.

SECOND LIEUT.
COCKBURN J.
COOPER R.
CROFT J. A. C.
HILL H. T.
HUNT R. F.
RICARD F.

COY. SJT. MAJOR
HOSKINS H.
LUCAS B., M.M.

COY. QMR. SERJT.
JONES W.
MONTGOMERY F. T., D.C.M.

SERJEANT
BUCKLEY T.
CHARLES A. E.
CLINTON J. T.
CRANBROOK W.
GARVEY J. A. G.
GATELEY J.
HICKS O. J.
HOLDEN H. H. B.
JEYNES E. T.
LUCKMAN W.
MORTON A.
PALMER F. S.
REEVES S. A.
SKIDMORE W. H.
SMITH. H.
STURT N. H.
TODD E.
WEST T.
WOODING F. C.

LANCE SERJEANT
BANNARD B. C.
BICKLEY A.
MULLISS S.
O'CALLAGHAN J. M.

CORPORAL
BRUSH A.

WHITEHEAD J.
WHITFIELD D.
WHITFIELD F. H.
WHITTIKER J. H.
WILES W.
WILKIE C.
WILKIN J.
WILKINS G. V.
WILKINS J. W.
WILKINSON H.
WILKINSON M.
WILKS T.
WILLETT W.

LANCE CORPORAL
ROBBINS T.
ROSSINDALE H.
SANDERS E.
SAWARD C.
SCULL J. P.
SUMNER W.
URQUHART C.
VERNER D.
WEEKS W. A.

PRIVATE
ADAMS C. H.
ADCOCK W.
ALLEN A.
AMEY W.
ANDREWS A.
ANDREWS G.
ANGUS D.
ARMFIELD J.
ASSINDER C. W.
ASTELL B. T.
ATKINS A.
AUSTIN J.
BACON J.
BAILEY C. W.
BAKER E. P.
BAKER T.
BAKER W.
BALDWIN G. D.
BALL J. J.
BALLARD E.
BAMFORD J. P.
BARCLAY A.
BAREFOOT C. H.
BARLEY F.
BARNETT E. W.
BARNETT G.
BARRATT F.
BASTABLE W. H.
BATSFORD W.
BATTIN C.
BAUGH J.
BAYLISS F.
BAYLISS H.
BEACH C. T.
BEALE J. A.
BEAUFOY B.
BEESLEY G. L.
BEESLEY J. E.
BEMBRIDGE H.
BENJAMIN H.W.
BIFFIN A. S.
BILKE B.
BIRD G. A.
BIRD J.
BLICK W. J.
BONEHILL D.
BONNER B.
BOSWORTH W.
BOULTON S. J.
BOUSFIELD S. R.
BOXWELL A. F.
BRACEY F.
BRADBURY E.
BRADSHAW A.
BRADSHAW L.
BRIMBLE R.
BROADFIELD O.
BROWN B.
BROWN C.

WRAY J. W.
WRIGHT J.
WRIGHT T.
WRIGHT T. B.
WYMER J. E.
WYNN W.
YEARHAM T.
YOUNG A. S.
YOUNG J.
YOUNG R.
YOUNGER J. 2169
YOUNGER J. 2667

PRIVATE
DAVIES W.
DAWSON W.
DEELEY J.
DENNIS W.
DOBBS R.
DOBINSON W.
DOUGHTY J.H.
DRENNON R.
DUCKERIN F. W.
EADON H.
EDWARDS J.
ELLIS A. H.
ELLIS G. H.
ELMS H.R.
EMMS W. T.
FALLON J.
FANE E. J.
FAULKNER J.
FEIST J.
FINCH W.
FISHER W. E.
FLETCHER E. A.
FLETCHER W.
FODEN H. H.
FOSTER L.
FOX T.
FRASER H.
FREEMAN C. E.
FREEMAN J.
GAHAN L.
GALLOWAY J.
GARDNER A. J.
GARLAND W.
GARLAND W. E.
GARTENFIELD C. R.
GARVEY W. H.
GEAR C. J.
GIBSON A.
GIFFORD W. H.
GILBERT J.
GILBERT J.
GILDERSON W. C.
GODRIDGE J.
GOLDING H. J.
GOODCHILD J. A.
GOODFIELD C.
GOODWIN A.
GOODYEAR J.
GORDON W. P.
GOUGH B. G.
GOVETT A. B.
GRAY W. C. H. E.
GREATRIX W.
GREENING A.
GREENWAY E. W.
GRIFFIN A.
GRIFFITHS A.
GRIFFITHS H.
HALL C.
HALL H.
HAMMOND J.
HANCOX C. J.
HANSON C.
HARRIS W. C.
HART J. T.
HASTINGS J. C.
HATELEY S.
HAWKES F. G.
HAYWOOD W.

NEWMAN R. H.
NICHOLLS A.
NICHOLLS E. A.
NOON W.
NORBURY A.
O'BRIEN T.
O'DELL F.
O'DOWD M.
OLIVER F.
OSBORNE J.
OVERY A.
OWEN G. E.
PACKER J.
PAPWORTH C. W.
PARKER E.
PARKER H.
PARKES F.
PARSONS H. E.
PASTON C.
PAYBODY H.
PEARSON J. W.
PERKINS H.
PERKS J. F.
PERRIN P.
PHILLIPS A.
PHILLIPS W.
PHILLIPSON F. K.
PICKARD T.
PIPER E. A.
PITT A. C.
POOLE M.
POTTER H.
PREEDY J. T.
PRESTON A.
SERVED AS
KERSHAW A.
PRICE E.
PRICE H.W.
PRIEST J. E.
PROBERT A. J.
PRYCE D. O'C.
RACHEL G.
RAWLINS B.
RAYSON H.
READ G. E.
RICHARDSON C. J.
ROBERTS G.
ROBERTS G. H.
ROBERTS J.
ROBERTS W.
ROBINSON W.
ROCHESTER C.
RODDS F.
ROONEY W.
ROWLEY J. J.
RYAN J. M.
SABELL S.
SAVAGE J. P.
SAWYER A.
SELBY W.

YATES W.

THE ROYAL FUSILIERS

LIEUT COLONEL
BIRCHALL A P D

CAPTAIN
BURDETT W.A.M.C.
CURWEN W. J. H.
DAY F. C.
De TRAFFORD T. C.
DOUDNEY H. D.
FORSTER H C
FRIEDBERGER W. S.
FULLER D M.M.C.
GRAY H. McK.
HARTER C. J.
HODGSON M. R. K.
MOXON G. J. M.
PUZEY A. K.
THOMAS-O'DONEL G. O. D. E. M.C.

LIEUTENANT
BERRILL B. F. G.

STIRK
STORER
STRINGE
SULLIVA
SURCH T
SWAIN
TAPP W
THOMAS
THOMAS
THOMPS
THORNH
TOON W
TOOTH
TOPPING
TORDOF
TRANTE
TRENCH
TRUDGE
TURVEY
TWYNHA
UNDERW
VALLAN
VARLEY
VARNEY
VINNICC
WAGSTA
WALDRO
WALKER
WALKER
WALTON
WARD C
WARD R
WARD S
WARING
WATKINS
WATKINS
WATTS
WATTS
WEARIN
WEAVER
WEBSTE
WEEDON
WESTON
WHARTO
WHEELE
WHITE C
WHITE
WILDE J
WILKINS
WILKINS
WILKSH
WILLIAM
WILSON
WILSON
WISE J.
WOODCO
WOODC
WOOLLI
WORROL
WRAGG
WRIGHT

YATES W.

THE ROYAL FUSILI
SECON
PERRIER
PRICE H
SCOTT V
SEALY C
SHOESM
SMITH J
STOLLE
STOVOL
TOTHIL
UNDERY
YOUNG

COY. SJT
CHILTON
CONNOLL
HAZELL
SMITH A

SER.
BARTLET
BERRY V

Many of the soldiers who fraternised with the Germans over Christmas were killed during the 2nd Battle of Ypres in April 1915 when the Germans used gas for the first time. Among the names of 54,400 commemorated on the Ypres (Menin Gate) Memorial are batman Private William Tapp and his officer Lieutenant Tillyer of the 1/ Royal Warwicks J Kerr

The Ypres (Menin Gate) Memorial was unveiled in 1927, designed by Sir Reginald Blomfield and the sculpture by Sir William Reid-Dick

J Kerr